POWER UP
YOUR PARENTING

A Practical Guide for Parenting Preteen and Teen Girls

ERICA ROOD, M.A.Ed.
ILLUSTRATIONS BY SHINHAE KANG

DEDICATIONS:

This book is dedicated to my family,
friends, and mentors, without whose
guidance, encouragement, and inspiration,
I would not be where I am today.
—Erica Rood

To my loving family, especially my amazing mother
who is my biggest supporter, and best friend.
—Karin "Shinhae" Kang

Philanthropy:
A portion of sales from this book will be
donated to San Pasqual Academy.

Acknowledgements:
Colleen Ster, for her unwavering dedication
and support of me and this book.

My partner in life, Majid Nikzad, for bringing joy,
adventure, and love every step of the way.

Linda Sorkin, for opening doors that
led me to where I am today.

Tami Walsh and Diana Sterling, for
sharing their experience and knowledge
of coaching families, parents, and teens.

John Mann, for his expert editing.

My parents, Carol Landale and Dave Rood, for
encouraging me to follow my heart and pursue my passion.

My wonderful clients, past, present, and future,
for inspiring me with their truths and wisdom.

Student Editorial Team: Lily Freeman, Isabella Kwon, Karin
Shinhae Kang, Alexandra Ster, Caroline Ster, and Isabelle Ster

Praise for *Power Up Your Parenting*

"Thank you Erica for taking the time to teach parents the wisdom and compassion you bring to your coaching. The book enables parents to step into the shoes of their daughter's coach through relatable examples and pragmatic solutions."
–Celia Szczuka, San Diego, CA

"Informative and practical. This book is just what my family needed. It is obvious Erica has seen first hand the challenges today's teens and parents are facing in this ever-changing, connected world. I am looking forward to incorporating these techniques into my day-to-day parenting in hopes of raising two confident, self-aware, and most importantly, happy daughters."
–Wendy Schott, Denver, NC

"Great ideas, tips, and tricks to engage our daughters in finding their authentic selves. Erica is helping engineer a whole generation of parents who support and empower the individuality of today's teens."
–Jennifer Kaufman, Larkspur, CO

"I found *Power Up Your Parenting* to be refreshingly accessible. It doesn't blame or judge parent and teen struggles, rather, it offers practical suggestions to move through the tumultuous teen years together as a caring team. Erica provides thoughtful approaches combined with sound reasoning of their effectiveness. She helps get the parent in shape so they can gently and with understanding, meet their teen where they are at and mindfully steer them through these challenging years. Erica includes relatable real-life examples from her years of experience, guiding parents and teens to achieve loving, working relationships."
–Sarah Mann, Milwaukee, WI

"*Power Up Your Parenting* has many tools for parents to help their daughters navigate the social, emotional, and academic challenges of being a teen. Erica Rood's approach is conversational, practical, and down-to-earth. She affirms a relationship between parents and their teenage daughters that embodies empathy, gratitude, structure, support, and open communications."
–Julie Watts, San Diego, CA

"*Power Up Your Parenting* has numerous techniques and insight on how to best approach some of the hard discussions that parents need to have with their teenage daughter."
–Chad Freeman, Castle Rock, CO

"As a mother of two teenage daughters, I'm always looking to find ways to positively connect with them in the limited time allowed in our busy lives of work, school, activities, friends, etc. *Power Up Your Parenting* teaches how to parent not from a place of fear or worry, but from a place of empathy and respect for our teenagers. The relationship building exercises incorporated into the book are also wonderful guides, not just to read and learn, but to act. Thank you Erica for the amazing book!"
–Christine Kang, San Diego, CA

"*Power Up Your Parenting* outlines a practical and compassionate approach to parenting teens. Erica offers a unique perspective for guiding teens through various challenges. As a father of three girls, I found the book extremely helpful and insightful! Thank you, Erica."
–Mike Nikzad, Dallas, TX

"The teen years can be the most difficult of a person's life and cause fear and a sense of lack of control in parents. The tools and practices in Erica's *Power Up Your Parenting* book give hope and practical applications to gain control in the most vulnerable season of life. This book will help teens and parents not just survive the teen years, it will empower them to be better humans and make the world a better place."
–Lynette Sanchez, San Diego, CA

"*Power Up Your Parenting* by Erica Rood is a wonderful book, tool, and reference guide for parents of teens and preteens. Now that I have read the book cover to cover, I plan on referring to this as needed and keeping it bedside until both of my girls are in college. I love that there is information for parents, teens, and activities for both. Growing up in today's crazy world is overwhelming, and watching my daughters navigate things I never had to deal with as a child is doubly so. I'm thankful to have a book with straight talk, steps, and advice that is clear and concise."
-Natalie Chiles, San Diego, CA

How and Why This Book Works

This book is like having a parent-coach in the palm of your hand. It is your guide to new parenting approaches that foster a strong connection and promote your teen's personal, social, and academic success. You will find solutions to the most common parenting concerns and teen challenges, plus gain practical strategies for supporting your teen in growing from good to great.

When you "Power Up Your Parenting," you approach your teen from a place of perspective rather than panic. Your teen feels capable, supported, and will respond to you positively rather than with defiance.

This book is divided into five sections:

1. Staying Connected
2. The Social World of Teens
3. The Academic World of Teens
4. Personal Growth
5. Tools for Life

At the end of each section there is a place for you to summarize your learning and consider how you will integrate the new parenting approaches into your everyday interactions. The 4114U Section: Tools for Teens includes a variety of activities that you can offer your teen or use with her.

Please keep in mind that the contents of this book is not intended to be a substitute for any professional medical advice, diagnosis, or treatment. I hope you will enjoy Power Up Your Parenting!

Erica Rood, M.A.Ed.
Life Coach for Parents, Teens, and Young Adults

Published by Reflections Publishing
© 2020 Reflections Publishing

All rights reserved. No part of this book may be used or reproduced in any manner whatsoever without the prior written permission of the publisher, except for brief quotations embodied in critical articles and reviews.

Neither the publisher nor the author are engaged in rendering professional medical advice or services to the individual reader. The ideas, procedures, and suggestions contained in this book are not intended as a substitute for consulting with your physician. All matters regarding your health require medical supervision. Neither the author nor the publisher shall be liable or responsible for any loss or damage allegedly arising from any information or suggestions in this book.

Names, characters, businesses, organizations, places, events, and incidents either are the product of the author's imagination or are used fictitiously. Any resemblance to actual persons, living or dead, events, or locales is entirely coincidental.

While the author has made every effort to provide accurate telephone numbers and Internet addresses at the time of publication, neither the publisher nor the author assume any responsibility for errors, or for changes that occur after publication. Further, the publisher does not have any control over and does not assume any responsibility for author or third party websites or their content.

First Edition. Published in the United States of America.

ISBN 978-1-61660-014-3

Visit our website at www.reflectionspublishing.com for more information or inquiries.

* * *

Table of Contents

About the Author	5
Introduction	7
Section One: Staying Connected	**10**
• Communicating With Your Teen	11
Section Two: The Social World of Teens	**20**
• Friend Challenges	21
• Bullying and Cyberbullying	24
• Popularity and Fitting In	28
• Social Media and Technology	32
• Partying, Experimenting, and Peer Pressure	38
Section Three: The Academic World of Teens	**46**
• Tackling Procrastination and Inspiring Motivation	47
• Minimizing Pressure and Supporting Success	53
Section Four: Personal Growth	**62**
• Supporting a Healthy Self-Esteem	63
• Nurturing an Authentic Self	67
• Uncovering a Passion	71
• Thriving Through Change	75
• Developing Leadership Skills	78
Section Five: Tools for Life	**84**
• Responsibility	85
• Grit and Resilience	88
• Compassion and Gratitude	91
Conclusion	**97**
4114U: Tools for Teens	**100**
Questions for Contemplation	**131**
Reference and Resources	**135**
4114U Concepts (Index)	**137**

About Erica, Your Parent-Coach

Ever since I can remember, I have been drawn to working with young people. I have volunteered at youth shelters and served as an educator in American and international schools. Now, I offer a very unique blend of coaching and teaching to girls and parents with the goal of raising wise, confident, and motivated young women.

During my years in the classroom, girls would often confide in me, sharing their personal struggles with body image, self-esteem, friendships, family dynamics, and school. They were afraid to turn to their parents for fear of being misunderstood and they did not want to turn to their friends for fear that their innermost feelings would become gossip. Too often, they felt alone and unsure. I did my best to guide and advise, but always felt restricted by time and requirements to cover core curriculum. I wanted to do more to help my students understand themselves and feel confident in handling the unique challenges they were facing.

Shortly after writing my master's thesis on relational aggression, which included a curriculum to teach girls about building their emotional intelligence and handling social challenges, I heard about a career called Teen Life Coaching. It was described as a field devoted to self-discovery, action, and accountability. A profession that focuses on building a client's personal strengths, ability to set and achieve goals, overcome obstacles, and ultimately move forward with confidence and intention. I thought, "This is it!"

In 2012, I took a risk. I left my full-time teaching job, became a certified Teen Wisdom™ Teen Life Coach, and started my coaching practice with a focus on preteen and teen girls. During my first year of coaching, I became acutely aware that parents were also struggling. They were exhausted, frustrated, and extremely worried that their daughters might go down the wrong path. More often than not, their parent lens clouded their ability to fully understand what their daughter was going through and support her in a meaningful way. I realized both teens and parents needed new tools and a fresh perspective. I added a parent-coaching component to my coaching programs and noticed that when parents took a different approach, they experienced positive changes in their relationship with their teen.

POWER UP YOUR PARENTING
A Practical Guide for Parenting Preteen and Teen Girls

INTRODUCTION

If you are parenting a teen daughter, chances are you have spent a night or two worrying. Perhaps you have talked with your friends about her outrageous behavior or quiet withdrawal. You have likely fought with her over homework, chores, respect, or following basic rules.

While it may feel as if worry and frustration dominate the teen years, there are also those moments of meaningful connection. There are feelings of awe and amazement when your daughter takes on new challenges in school or sports and succeeds. You have celebrated wins and supported her through unexpected change. You have relished those times when she confided in you, demonstrating her trust that you will understand her secrets and answer her most personal questions.

Although she may not show it, your daughter deeply appreciates and craves those moments. As she navigates the path to independence and explores what it means to be an individual, she relies on you for support, understanding, and guidance. She needs your consistency, calm, strength, and reassurance that who she is now is not who she is going to be. She needs you to coach, guide, teach, and parent in a new way. A way that leaves her feeling inspired, capable, accountable, and proud of who she is becoming.

Teens Need a New Kind of Parent

Although the teen years are rife with extremes, you do not have to feel as if you are walking on eggshells or bracing yourself until high school graduation. When you change your approach to your teen, you can maximize the opportunities for meaningful connection and peaceful communication.

Over the years, I have coached hundreds of preteen and teenage girls. Through many conversations with them, it has become clear what they need and want from their parents:

- Teens want their parents to listen and understand.

- Teens require boundaries, consistency, and encouragement. They need to feel capable and proud of who they are and who they are becoming.

- Teens need their parents to teach, coach, and guide them toward their highest potential.

SECTION ONE:

STAYING CONNECTED

COMMUNICATING WITH YOUR TEEN

Teenagers think they are ready to take the world by storm. They want to make their own decisions and play by their own rules. They tend to think they can do everything on their own and the last thing they need is help from their parents.

At their best, the teen years are a time of exciting change, growth, and new discoveries. At their worst, they are years filled with arguing, tension, and disconnection.

Most teens share a common complaint: my parents just don't understand. Equally, many parents express their puzzlement with their teen and wonder what happened to their sweet little one.

> ## PARENTS - UGH!
>
> At our first meeting, Angela relaxed on the chair in my office. Her bright pink nails combed through her hair and she rolled her eyes as she described her parents. "I mean they are just so annoying. They don't let me do anything!" She went on, "And my mom... UGH! She just gets SO weird when she tries to talk to me about anything personal... like sex or stuff like that. I just can't talk to her about anything without her turning it into a huge thing."
>
> She shuddered and went on to describe how uncomfortable and difficult it was for her to have any type of meaningful conversation with her parents.
>
>

The truth is, in spite of their outward show of indifference, teenagers actually want their parents' support and guidance. They expect their parents to play a pivotal role in their lives. They long to feel that they can ask questions and talk about problems, hopes, and dreams with the family members who are closest to their hearts.

So, how do you effectively maintain a healthy and communicative bond with your freedom-craving teenager?

Ask open-ended questions and listen without judgment.

Open-ended questions are like invitations. They usually start with the word "what" and evoke contemplation and reflection. Your daughter may choose to respond to your questions or not, but either way, honor her response. Do not interrupt or assume your advice is needed. Instead, consider asking if your opinion or assistance would be helpful.

SAY THIS...	NOT THAT...
What was the best part of your day?	How was your day?
What was that like for you?	Why did you do that?
What support do you need?	Do you need my help?
What are your options right now?	Here is what you can do...

 Set and maintain clear boundaries and expectations for behavior.

Teens notoriously test the boundaries, so it is important to know your bottom line and state it clearly. Your bottom line is what you really want for your teen. When you have determined your bottom line, consider whether or not it is negotiable. If it is not, tell your teen this is a non-negotiable expectation or rule. If it is, engage your teen in a respectful discussion about expectations until you reach an agreement for behavior. Talk about accountability and make the consequences crystal clear.

#3 Show your respect.

Be sure to say, "I respect you/your..." frequently. Follow it with a quality or strength that you genuinely admire, rather than an accomplishment. When you highlight your daughter's skills or qualities over her accomplishments, she will feel seen and truly understood. She will become more receptive and willing to engage in conversations.

SAY THIS...	NOT THAT...
I really respect your patience toward your brother.	I wish you could be patient more often.
I respect your dedication to school and commitment to studying.	I am so proud of you for earning good grades.
I admire your ability to listen and be fair with your friends.	When I was your age, I had to do the same thing.

#4 Check yourself.

Your words, actions, and tone are major influences on your teen's behavior. Words have the power to take a relationship from loving and connected to closed and aggressive. Be mindful of how you express your concerns.

* * *

Maintaining a trusting and open relationship with your teen takes effort and awareness. There is no one-size-fits-all guide to parenting, but listening, showing respect, and staying mindful are building blocks to any healthy relationship. For a teen, these approaches foster feelings of being understood and accepted. When your daughter feels understood and accepted, the walls go down and you are able to sustain a strong, balanced, and connected relationship throughout life.

In addition to parents, teens need other trusted adults in their inner circle. As they become more independent, they look to people outside their family for support, encouragement, or advice. Creating a strong network of support can benefit everyone. Parents breathe a sigh of relief knowing their daughter has a safe and trustworthy support system and teens know there are people to turn to when they don't want to open up to their friends or parents.

SAY THIS...NOT THAT...

SAY THIS...

I'm really concerned about your performance in school. Your grades have been slipping since December. What support do you need?

NOT THAT...

Your grades have been slipping since December! You aren't putting any effort into homework! That's it – no phone until you bring your grades up.

PUTTING IT ALL TOGETHER

What do you now understand about staying connected to your teen?

_____
_____
_____
_____
_____
_____
_____
_____
_____
_____
_____
_____
_____
_____
_____
_____
_____
_____
_____
_____
_____
_____
_____
_____

How will you begin to parent differently?

_____
_____
_____
_____
_____
_____
_____
_____
_____
_____
_____
_____
_____
_____
_____
_____
_____
_____
_____
_____
_____
_____
_____

- Make sure to share you newly found knowledge!

SECTION TWO:

THE SOCIAL WORLD OF TEENS

FRIEND CHALLENGES

During the teen years, friendships are a primary source of happiness, security, and identity. For girls, friendships can be unsteady and changeable. It is not unusual for girls to use friendship as a weapon. If your daughter finds herself in a friendship plagued by covert aggression, she is likely to feel bewildered and sad, believing that it is her fault that her "friends" have suddenly turned against her. Unless she feels safe enough to open up to you, you are likely going to see her avoiding social activities and finding excuses to skip school.

GIRL DRAMA

Erin had a history of "girl-drama." In middle school, the girls she thought were her friends started to randomly make fun of her and leave her out. Understandably, she was desperate to know why. Using social media as her shield, she would inquire tirelessly: "What's wrong?" "Why aren't you including me?" "What did I do?" Sometimes the girls would respond with cold, curt responses and deny any wrongdoing, which would make Erin feel crazy. Other times, they were straight-up mean, telling her she was annoying and lied all the time. Erin found herself in a losing war of insults and mean-spirited comments with a group she thought were her friends. Yet, no matter how mean they were to her, she could not let them go. She did not want to move on.

Because Erin did not open up to her parents, they were bewildered by her sadness and frequent requests to stay home from school or skip practice. They worried and wanted to know how to help.

When girls are going through so-called friend drama, they have an opportunity to learn how to deal with difficult people, strengthen their sense of self, and define what is important in a friend. As always, parents play a key role in coaching their teen through friend challenges. These four parenting practices will help your teen develop social-awareness and cultivate healthy friendships.

 Model positive relationships and calm conflict resolution.

Consider how your friendships show your daughter how to handle change and challenge. How do you and your friends support each other and lift each other up? How do you resolve conflicts?

 Talk about characteristics of friends.

Ask her how she defines a best friend, good friend, and pretty good friend. When you engage in discussions, or simply "think aloud" about your own relationships, you are providing your daughter with a framework for healthy friendships and teaching her language that will help her understand her different types of friends.

List the pros and cons of a friendship full of ups and downs.

If your daughter is on the brink or in the thick of friend drama, writing or talking out the pros and cons of a friendship can help her get to the bottom of the issue and determine her best next steps.

 Identify qualities of friendships that make her feel good and those that do not.

This conversation can easily follow creating a list of pros and cons. You can also point out the qualities that make your daughter a good friend and ask her what she values and expects from those whom she calls friends.

* * *

Never underestimate the impact and importance of your teen's social world. When you see your teen struggling, do your best to offer nonjudgmental support and open-hearted listening. Use the challenge as an opportunity for her to learn important lessons about friendships, social-awareness, and resilience.

BULLYING AND CYBERBULLYING

Despite the plethora of anti-bullying campaigns, bullying continues to be a widespread problem for youth. It is fairly common for friend drama to be confused with bullying, but there is an important difference. Bullying is repetitive and continues over an extended period of time. Bullying can be more blatant and even physical, whereas friend drama is often hard to detect and usually shows up in the form of gossip and exclusion. Both can be devastating and both require parent support.

FAKE NEWS

Sarah is a sixth-grade girl who uses social media ... a lot! She uses the site to share her favorite photos and connect with her friends. On the outside, Sarah's profile is harmless. She highlights her skills as a surfer, shares cheerful pictures of herself with friends, and includes plenty of selfies. Unfortunately, Sarah has another use for social media. She uses the platform to harass, threaten, and name-call her friends. No one knows that the comments they are reading are coming from her because she created a fake account under a completely different name. When Sarah logs onto this account, she takes on a different persona. She feels powerful and protected behind the shield of her screen.

Bullying has been around for generations, but cyberbullying is a new phenomenon that many parents feel ill-equipped to handle. The following ideas can help with different forms of bullying.

 Raise your social-media awareness.

Learn about the latest apps and websites used by your preteen/teen. When you are empowered with information, you can better understand and support your daughter. Do not be afraid to start the conversation early. Talk about the potential dangers that exist on social media and set appropriate boundaries.

#2 Strengthen individuality.

Celebrate what makes your daughter unique. Regular recognition of strengths and talents boosts self-esteem. When teen girls are clear and confident in themselves, they are less likely to bully or be bullied and more able to stand up for themselves and others. Self-esteem is also tied to resilience—which is the ability to bounce back from adversity.

 Foster supportive relationships.

The parent-teen relationship is a model for all other relationships. It provides a framework for the developing teen to deal with emotions, conflict, and differences. Adolescents who have strong, supportive family relationships are more willing to ask for help, more able to handle conflicts, and they tend to choose supportive, compassionate friends.

#4 **Boost competence.**

Be a model for respectful, confident social interactions. Your daughter will learn how to self-advocate by watching you. Take time to directly teach her how to be assertive through body language and words: encourage sitting up tall, making eye contact, walking with confidence, and choosing clear, bold words.

BOOST COMPETENCE

- **BE ASSERTIVE**
  - Speak up
  - Make eye contact
  - Use clear, bold words

- **BODY LANGUAGE**
  - Stand tall
  - Heart lifted
  - Eyes forward

#5 Model and teach empathy.

Share your own feelings and difficult experiences. It is important for your teen to see that you are human too. Use real-life experiences, books, and TV shows to spark conversations about how other people feel and why. Help your teen step into other people's shoes and stretch her capacity to understand their perspective.

* * *

The sad truth is that bullying and cyberbullying are not going to go away. The good news is that parents, teachers, and coaches can take mindful action to promote resilience, empathy, and self-advocacy skills.

POPULARITY AND FITTING IN

When you are a teen girl, popularity matters… a lot.

Girls derive a great deal of self-worth from their friends. They rely on their friends for validation, acceptance, and camaraderie. Being "popular" takes on a high degree of importance. In fact, many teens believe being popular equates to being happy, and they will do whatever it takes to fit in.

ANYTHING TO BE POPULAR

In middle school, Julie had a lot of friends, but once she started high school things began to change. Her close-knit group grew fragmented as each girl got involved in different sports and met new friends. Two of the girls who used to be her "besties" started hanging out with the "popular girls." They began dressing differently, expressing interest in boys, and partying. Julie began to feel more and more the outsider.

During her first coaching session, she opened up easily and expressed her dilemma. She wanted to maintain her middle-school friendships and fit in with the popular group, but she was not sure how much, if anything, she had in common with the group. She felt she would have to compromise her values and interests in order to be accepted and she worried that if she didn't, she would be a social outcast or isolated for the rest of high school. She was also angry because she saw her two best friends changing and she felt this was all for the sake of being liked.

WHAT'S WRONG WITH ME?

Arianna was a sweet, yet shy, 11-year-old. She struggled with academics and friends. Throughout her elementary-school years, she had been relentlessly taunted and teased. At one point, it became so bad that her parents moved her to a new school. There, she tried desperately to find a best friend only to find that the girls were already paired. "No one wants to be my friend," she explained to me with eyes full of tears. Arianna started to question herself. She wondered what was wrong with her and why she could not find a friend.

It can be confusing and heartbreaking to watch your daughter struggle with making friends or move away from her core values for the sake of fitting in. Although you have less and less control over your teen daughter's social world, you can serve as her parent-coach, guiding and supporting her in understanding the difference between having friends and being popular.

 Affirm her strengths and values.

Despite their natural tendency to test the boundaries and resist parental influence, teens have a deep desire and need to receive affirmations from the adults in their lives. This means looking beyond their accomplishments and praising them for who they are, rather than what they do. When your teen receives respectful acknowledgements, her sense of self strengthens and she will be less inclined to rely on others for validation.

Outline the differences between popularity and friendship.

Debunk the myth that being popular means being happy. Ask:
- *What does it mean to be a friend?*
- *What do you value in a friendship?*
- *What are the qualities of a true friend?*

Challenge your teen to consider the problems with popularity. Very often being popular requires teens to behave in a certain way, rather than exploring and sharing their authentic self. Help broaden her perspective and understanding of popularity versus genuine friendship.

 Honor her feelings.

As insignificant as it may seem to you, friend drama provokes powerful feelings in your teen. When feelings of disappointment, sadness, anger, or loneliness surface, offer acknowledgment and validation. Remind your teen that you are available and ready to listen when she is ready to share. When a conversation is sparked, ask open-ended questions that illuminate solutions and best next steps. Demonstrate your understanding, through listening and encouraging.

Questions to Try:
- What do you think is your best next step?
- What can you do right now to address the situation?
- Is there another way to experience this situation?
- Would you like to tell me more?

* * *

Be patient as you help your teen understand popularity and how to be true to her values. Allow her time to draw her own conclusions and take actions to develop friendships, which allow her to be true to herself.

SOCIAL MEDIA AND TECHNOLOGY

Many parents wonder how to best manage their teen's screen time and activity on social media.

Parents frequently ask:
- *How much screen time is too much?*
- *What are the best ways to manage social media?*
- *Is it okay to check my teen's phone?*

When it comes to social media and technology, there is not a one-size-fits-all solution, but there are basic guidelines that will help your teen stay safe and responsible.

ADDICTED TO THE SCREEN

"I don't know what she does on her phone for hours." Lucie's mom sighed and went on to explain her struggle with managing her daughter's screen time. "As soon as she gets home, she's on her phone texting or watching YouTube and when it comes to time to start homework, she insists she needs her phone to complete her assignments. At dinner time, she begs to eat in her room so she can be on her phone, then she's up till the early morning hours glued to the screen." Lucie's mom was exasperated. When I asked about rules and limits on screen-time, she was quick to say none work, because Lucie is a "nightmare" when her phone is taken away.

Phones, tablets, and laptops are tools. Just like driving a car, they require a skill-set that includes responsibility, maturity, and an understanding of the rules and consequences. Before you provide your teen with a tech device, ensure that these qualities are strong and follow these parenting DOs and DON'Ts:

 Do make your rules and expectations clear.

Before your teen has access to a phone, tablet, or laptop, set up clear parameters and outline fair consequences for misuse. Talk about the dangers that exist online: offensive content, predators, and a lasting digital footprint.

 Do talk about and model healthy relationship skills online and offline.

These include empathy, honesty, understanding and accepting differences, and resolving conflicts appropriately. Talk about how sometimes, when we communicate over a screen, we lose sight of the fact that there is a real person on the other side. Without seeing the real person, it can be easy to discount or misunderstand her feelings. Harsh words are easier to use. Help your daughter understand the elements of a healthy relationship, so she will be less likely to get involved in online abuse.

#3 Do ask open-ended questions.

Frame your questions in a way that encourages your daughter to discern the important differences between online and real-life interactions. During these conversations, listen with an open mind and intention of understanding what attracts her to certain people or certain sites. This information will help guide your parenting and conversations on responsible internet use.

Questions to Try:

- Would this conversation be different in person?
- What is this person like in "real-life?"
- How would it feel to say that face-to-face?
- Is this something you need to address now or can you give yourself some time to think about your best next steps?

Do teach the difference between reacting and responding.

Social media encourages an already impulsive teen to be even more impulsive. Teach your daughter the differences between reacting and responding. Encourage thoughtful responses or no response at all to messages that incite emotional reactions.

REACTION	RESPONSE
• Reactions are usually done without forethought. • They are automatic.	• Responses are thoughtful and deliberate. A response usually requires time to process initial feelings, think through optimal outcomes, and determine best next steps.

 Do reserve the right to check her phone.

When your parenting radar goes up and your instincts are telling you that something is not right, have a conversation with your teen and tell her that you are going to need to check her device.

 **Don't pry!**

While you are the owner of the device, and therefore have the right to check it, do so only when you have valid reason or concern. If you check too often, it sends the message of distrust and invasion of her privacy.

 Don't be afraid to set limits on screen time.

It is totally appropriate to take away a device at a reasonable bedtime hour and set time limits for screen time during waking hours. Keep in mind that many homework assignments require technology.

 Don't give your teen free access to the Internet.

Find out about parental controls, ISPs, filters, and systems for monitoring your teen's talk time and social connections.

 Don't treat the phone, screen, or laptop as a requirement.

It is a privilege to have these devices. They can make life easier and more fun, but they are not necessities. As with any privilege, make sure your teen demonstrates maturity and readiness to handle each device.

#10 Don't make social media the enemy.

Yes, there is a lot of negative content available on social media sites, and there are undeniable dangers, but social media is an important lifeline for your teen. It is a valued platform for connection, self-discovery, and personal expression. Instead of blaming social media and parenting from a place of worry and fear, set up reasonable limits, keep lines of the communication open about the challenges and dangers of social media, and foster your teen's sense of responsibility and trust.

* * *

Screens are not going away and social media activity is becoming more and more widespread. Educate yourself so you can calibrate with your teen. Have her educate you on her cyber world and then guide her to use technology and social media appropriately and safely.

PARTYING, EXPERIMENTING, AND PEER PRESSURE

During elementary and middle school, parties tend to have more structure. There is a playful theme with sugary treats and colorful decorations. During high school, parties become unstructured peer gatherings, often with little to no adult supervision. Sugary treats and colorful decorations are replaced with bottles of booze and bowls of mystery pills. So-called party games involve alcohol, tobacco, drugs, or sex. Despite their age, it is easy for teens to obtain alcohol and tobacco, and in many cases, it is even easier for them to get their hands on illegal and prescription drugs.

I PROMISE, I'LL NEVER DO IT AGAIN...

Hope was fifteen when her parents picked her up from a party, belligerent and incoherent. She could barely make her way to the car without falling over. Once home safely, she passed out on the couch, and her parents looked through her bag, discovering a vape pen and several pills that they later identified as Vicodin. She faced a strict punishment but a few months later, repeated the offense. This time, Hope's parents received a call from another parent who was concerned that Hope had encouraged her daughter to smoke marijuana. Hope's parents imposed another firm consequence and had a stern heart-to-heart with her. Through their conversations, Hope admitted to using alcohol and marijuana when out with friends. She promised she would stop, but her parents were not so sure.

Hope's parents sought me out in hopes that coaching would provide their daughter with decision-making skills and tools to handle the pressure to experiment with substances.

When I met Hope, she was guarded, but expressed a readiness for change. Her coaching sessions focused on self-discovery, planning for her future, and understanding why and how to make self-empowering choices. After several months of regular meetings and consistent follow-through at home, Hope turned a corner. She made a commitment to herself, her parents, and me that she would refrain from drinking and taking drugs. She made a new group of friends and shifted her focus from parties and fun to academic responsibilities and her future.

* * *

While parties can be a dangerous playing field for risky behavior, you do not need to ban them altogether. Instead, consider how to prepare your daughter to make smart, safe, and responsible choices when she is out with friends.

Outline clear expectations and consequences.

When it comes to alcohol, drugs, curfew, adult supervision, and communicating her whereabouts, make your expectations clear. Do not assume she already knows. Be simple and explicit in your rules and outline fair consequences should the rules be broken.

 Talk about drugs, tobacco, and alcohol... often!

Do not shy away from the hard and often awkward conversations about the damaging effects of drugs, tobacco, and alcohol. Provide your teen with information about addiction and abuse. Explain how drugs and alcohol impact her ability to make safe, wise decisions.

 Be consistent and firm.

Once you have made your rules and consequences clear, be consistent and firm. Let your teen know that you uphold a strict, non-negotiable policy.

 Design an exit strategy.

Talk with your daughter about what she should do if she finds herself in an unsafe or uncomfortable situation. Come up with a code word that can be used via text or phone call. Brainstorm different ways to say no and what to do if a friend is in need of help.

Be present, proactive, and informed.

Always tune in and calibrate with your teen. The more you understand her motivations and vulnerabilities, the easier it will be to detect a problem. Do not tell yourself that your teen cannot access drugs, tobacco, and alcohol. She can. They are readily available at school, online, and at popular teen hangout spots. Inform yourself of what substances and devices are trending with teens. Much of today's paraphernalia is designed to be concealable and mimic everyday devices like writing pens and flash drives. Also, drugs often go by cryptic nicknames like Molly, Spice, or bars. Find out what is trending.

 Deepen your understanding of peer pressure.

It is no secret that peers play an important role during the teen years. They have considerable influence when it comes to making decisions about partying or experimenting with drugs and alcohol. However, peer pressure does not exist in the form of threats or taunts. More and more teens tell me that when they say "no" to doing what everyone else is doing, no one really cares. The push to conform is more of a self-imposed pressure that stems from a teen's natural desire to fit in. To combat this, it is essential to build your teen's individuality, resilience, and inner strength. When she can stand in her power and truth, she will actually gain respect and make friends with those who recognize her ability to act as an individual.

* * *

Teens are going to experiment. They will explore different styles, hobbies, sports, and test the boundaries. It is all part of becoming independent. Teens who grow up in a household where boundaries are firm, support is unwavering, and respect and understanding are cornerstones, are more likely to make wise and thoughtful choices. This is especially true during the stage of risk-taking and experimentation.

PUTTING IT ALL TOGETHER

What do you now understand about your teen's social world?

How will you begin to parent differently?

_____

- Make sure to share you newly found knowledge!

SECTION THREE:

THE ACADEMIC WORLD OF TEENS

TACKLING PROCRASTINATION AND INSPIRING MOTIVATION

Students who have difficulty recognizing the value of education, or who fear academic failure, often take the easy way out. Rather than study for a test, or face the deadline to turn in an assignment, they opt for watching YouTube or Snap-chatting with a friend. As procrastination sets in, motivation diminishes.

Teens are still developing their ability to think ahead and, more importantly, work backward from their future dreams to their current reality. They need support in paving the way from where they are to where they want to be. The first step is to help them identify what matters to them now and why. From there, they can begin to discern which skills, habits, and mindsets are helpful in pushing them toward their dreams and which are taking them off track.

> **THE DOWNWARD SPIRAL**
>
> Andi was in the middle of tenth grade. While she expressed high hopes for her future, she had very little motivation for school and did not care that she was earning C's and D's. She allowed assignments to pile up, deadlines to come and go, and as a result, she fell so far behind that she thought the only solution was to give up. Her plan was to finish high school at a private continuation school. Her parents offered every support they could: academic tutors, consistent reminders, meetings with teachers, study groups, and even an education-organization expert (yes, those exist.) Nothing seemed to work. Their daughter was in danger of failing tenth grade.

Andi needed to develop a system that would support her school success and help her feel more in control. In addition to learning basic study skills and time management, she needed to understand the value of school. She needed to clarify why earning good grades mattered and how her grades would influence her ability to achieve her goals. As we discussed her plans for the future, she grew excited. She wanted what many teens want: fame, success, and wealth. Although vague, her goals provided a platform for exploring how they could be achieved. We started to work backwards, eventually getting to her present situation in tenth grade. She began to see that the classes she found meaningless were, in fact, stepping stones toward her ultimate desires. We outlined small steps she could take that would create a tangible change. As Andi started to take a different approach, her parents wanted to support her efforts. Since their previous attempts led to arguments and fights, they were not sure how to begin again.

#1 Make learning meaningful.

If your daughter's low motivation comes from a lack of interest in school, help her to see how the learning she does now is relevant to her goals for the future. She's likely to say something like, "I'll never use math. I want to be an actress!" or "Ms. Jones doesn't know how to teach and she doesn't like me." If this is the case, help her see a difficult class or teacher as an opportunity to learn how to handle challenging situations and people. Look for ways to promote a growth mindset. Help her see that the classes she perceives as meaningless and boring are actually stepping stones toward the life she dreams of living because they are helping her learn, grow, and develop essential life skills.

For the younger teen, make learning come alive: watch movies related to the "boring" subject, engage in conversations about the books she's reading, or visit museums to explore social studies and science concepts. Get creative with math concepts: show her their practical application through cooking, shopping, building, art, and sports. Always show your support and enthusiasm for the learning process. Emphasize the process over the product.

#2 Scaffold for success.

When assignments and deadlines pile up, teens are unable to find a way to overcome what feels like an insurmountable list of to-dos. They feel stuck and ill equipped to take the first step. Their solution is to put it off, to procrastinate.

Teens who procrastinate benefit from learning how to break down assignments into smaller tasks. Help your teen plan out when each small task must be accomplished. Teens usually work better when they have short bursts of work time, so try starting with 20-30 minute work periods. Set the timer, and for the first few weeks, monitor and acknowledge your teen's accomplishments – even sit beside her and do your own work. Keep in mind the end goal: to teach work habits that will lead to academic success.

#3 Create a support team.

Teens are good at rejecting their parents' well-meaning support. They may feel it as an additional pressure or it may be their way of showing their growing sense of independence. If your support is rejected, consider creating a support team to help your teen stay accountable and on track.

The team may include teachers, school counselors, therapists, coaches, or other trusted adults. It may also include one of your teen's friends, someone who has her best interests at heart and can be a responsible guide. The purpose of the team is to reinforce proactive work habits and provide feedback and encouragement. Team members point out how your teen can use her strengths to get through challenges that previously led to procrastination. Plan regular check-ins with your teen and her team and make sure she is asking for help when she needs it.

* * *

Maintaining your teen's motivation and minimizing procrastination requires a careful balance of support and rescue. It is tempting to jump in and save her: complete a homework assignment, help with a project, or write an excuse for late work. Over time, this only results in more procrastination and lack of motivation. If you begin to make learning meaningful, build a scaffold for success, and create a system of support, your teen will start to avoid the trap of procrastination, set her own goals, and effectively manage her time.

MOST COMMON PROCRASTINATION TRIGGERS AND SOLUTIONS

Most Common Procrastination Triggers	Solutions
1. Feeling overwhelmed	1. Help your teen break down tasks into smaller items.
2. Not knowing where to begin	2. Help your teen create a to-do list and choose the most urgent item.
3. Laziness	3. Help your teen connect with her purpose. (Try using: What's Behind Your Goals in the 4114U Section.)
4. Dislike of the subject	4. Help your teen see beyond the subject. For example, if she is not doing math homework because she doesn't like math, help her see the other skills she is practicing/strengthening by completing her math homework.
5. Distraction	5. Remove distractions and create a quiet work area.

MINIMIZING PRESSURE AND SUPPORTING SUCCESS

For today's high school students, academic stakes are high. Earning admission to college is difficult, even for the students who are not aiming to attend prestigious institutions. Consequently, teens put an enormous pressure on themselves to perform and achieve. They spend countless hours on homework. Test scores are status symbols. They are led to believe that acceptance into a top college is the only path to happiness and success. As early as middle school, students are preparing and worried about getting on the "right" college path. For many students, this pressure translates to feeling overwhelmed and leads to tidal waves of anxiety and stress.

JUGGLING LIFE

I met Tiffany at the end of her junior year of high school. She was a high-achieving, motivated student with an extremely full schedule. In addition to taking three AP classes at her rigorous school, she was involved in five clubs, three of which she was President, and played on the varsity volleyball team. She had a boyfriend and a strong group of friends, but spent very little time with them because almost all of her extra time was spent on her homework, clubs, or sports. Her parents were concerned that she did not get enough sleep and was growing increasingly irritable and moody. She would frequently stay up until 1 A.M. doing homework and when her parents offered reminders to start earlier, she would explode. Tiffany acknowledged she put a huge amount of pressure on herself and had high expectations of success. She also acknowledged that her stress level was typically an eight out of ten, on a good day! While reaching her academic goals and staying involved were essential for Tiffany, she was open to finding ways to stay motivated and directed while minimizing the level of overwhelming school stress she felt so often.

Like many teens, Tiffany needed effective strategies for managing her stress without sacrificing her dreams and goals.

Parents are usually the first to notice when their teen's stress reaches unhealthy levels: morning stomach aches, migraine headaches, overwhelming nervousness at bedtime, requests to skip school, or pleas to be home-schooled. While these are distressing experiences for you and your teen, it is important not to fall into the trap of rescuing. Although it may feel easier at the time, allowing her to skip school or giving in to complaints you know are caused by academic stress, are disservices to your teen. Instead, when your teen is under high levels of school stress, seize the opportunity to teach essential life skills.

Cultivate a "What if?" mindset.

Teens tend to have tunnel vision but, a "What if?" mindset will help broaden their perspective and make it easier to find ways to self-support and self-soothe during stressful periods. Encourage a "What if?" mindset by asking these questions:

- What would it be like if you were not stressed?

- What if you could have your ideal school year?

- What if you woke up every morning motivated and happy to go to school? How would it make your day different?

When your teen answers these questions, listen. Find what is reasonable and possible. Then, identify what action steps can be taken.

 **Create stress-busting routines.**

Many teens have a hard time identifying their stress triggers and even more do not know healthy ways to manage their triggers or reduce their stress. Make a T-chart on a piece of paper. Invite your teen to write all the things that stress her out on one side. As she does, validate her pain and frustration. This communicates a message that you understand. On the other side of the chart, ask her to list what she currently does to relieve stress. Then, together, add to this list. Think of new stress busters she can do on a regular basis to keep stress low.

Stress-Relieving Practices for Teens (and Parents)

- Weekly beach walk
- Family movie night
- Cooking and baking
- Painting
- Yoga
- Creative breathing, like the Bear Breath

How to do a Bear Breath:

Step One:
On the inhale breath, acknowledge how you feel.

Step Two:
At the top of the inhale, hold the breath and tighten all your muscles.

Step Three:
On the exhale breath, sigh (loudly) and repeat a personalized motivational statement, such as
- "I can do this!"
- "I can let go!"

#3 Build on her strengths.

While you believe in your daughter, she may need some help believing in herself. Teach her how to use her unique strengths and talents as tools. First, identify her strengths and inner qualities. For example, say, "I really admire your dedication to school. I respect you for staying the course even though things are not ideal right now. You have an ability to persevere." As you get in a regular habit of noticing the qualities that drive daily behaviors or accomplishments, she will start to see those qualities in herself. When the feelings of stress come tumbling in, ask her how she can use her strengths to get through the storm. This is a great time to come back to the "What if?" mindset by saying something like, "I wonder what would happen if you tapped into your ability to persevere. Do you think that could be helpful in this situation?"

#4 Reframe failure.

Highlight the fact that failures are opportunities for growth. Very often "failing" is an indication that we need to refocus or redirect. Failure is a valuable learning experience for teens and adults alike. Broaden your daughter's perspective around failure by asking open-ended questions like, "What could you do differently next time? or "What do you think this experience is teaching you?" Share your own experiences of failing and getting back up and find real-life examples that inspire and motivate your teen.

* * *

When your teen embraces an optimistic outlook, understands how to manage her stress, believes in herself, and reframes failure, she will be able to handle school stress, or any other stress, with ease.

PUTTING IT ALL TOGETHER

What do you now understand about your teen's academic world?

How will you begin to parent differently?

___

- Make sure to share you newly found knowledge!

SECTION FOUR:

PERSONAL GROWTH

PROMOTING A HEALTHY SELF-ESTEEM

Today, more than ever, teenage girls face an overwhelming pressure to be perfect. They believe they should have a perfect body, perfect skin, perfect hair, perfect grades, perfect friends, and a perfect life. Many girls are also driven to be at the top in academics and sports. Teens want it all and sometimes they work hard to make it look as if they do. However, outward appearances can be deceiving. Underneath the perceived perfection can be a girl who feels hollow, empty, and lost. These feelings are exacerbated by the tendency to compare. When girls scroll through Instagram or browse stories on Snapchat, they automatically size themselves up against a perceived ideal. Comparison leads them to put an even greater effort into appearing to be perfect.

NOT GOOD ENOUGH

Remi started coaching her freshman year of high school. She had a warm, vibrant energy, was a good student, and had a solid group of friends. On the outside, Remi appeared content, confident, and self-directed, but she was plagued by an inner voice that frequently told her she was not good enough. Sometimes this voice consumed her, causing emotional breakdowns or what she called "anxiety attacks." When we explored this inner voice, she would shift to the edge of her chair, legs crossed and arms like a shield. She admitted to feeling ugly and "fat." She frequently compared herself to the girls in her peer group whom she described as slim and strong and would lament that she would never have a body like theirs.

Like so many teenage girls, Remi was caught in a spiral of comparison and self-criticism, which led to debilitating self-doubt. In her coaching sessions, she learned how to tame the harmful thoughts of criticism and shift her doubtful thoughts to more helpful, constructive thoughts. She made a commitment to practice a new form of comparison; instead of focusing on qualities other people possessed that she felt she was missing, she would practice celebrating their gifts and beauty, while also celebrating her own.

When girls start placing a greater importance on how they look rather than who they are and what they are capable of, their self-worth weakens. When they compare themselves or strive toward an unrealistic and unattainable ideal image, their self-esteem plummets. Girls with low self-esteem are more likely to be reactive or defiant at home. They are less likely to offer opinions or speak up in class. They are more inclined to engage in harmful activities with friends.

If your daughter is caught in the downward spiral of comparison and self-doubt, she needs help in establishing a healthy sense of self. She needs to develop a shield against the constant stream of messages and images that promote perfection and challenge her self-worth.

#1 Be a positive role model.

Your attitude and actions contribute to your daughter's inner dialogue and inform the choices she will make in life. When you sigh each time you look in the mirror, or make subtle complaints about an extra pound, new wrinkle, or what you "really should not have" eaten, your teen starts to normalize self-criticism. Be mindful of how you talk about your body and yourself. Shift the language from one of criticism to one of acceptance. Shift the focus from outward appearances to inner qualities, character, and values.

#2 Talk about changes.

Talk with your teen about how her body is changing. When you have these conversations, use a tone of excitement and wonder. Remind her that she inhabits an amazing, extraordinary body. One that thrives when it is honored and respected.

#3 Help your teen make sense of the media.

Talk about the images in magazines, television, and the Internet. Share what you know about what it takes to get "picture perfect" and that it is impossible to live up to something that is not real.

Embrace the flaws. No one is perfect.

Celebrate each other's quirks and flaws. Laugh off the bad days.

Get moving with your daughter.

Dance, run, hike, or take a yoga class. Practice non-competitive, energizing activities together and talk about the amazing benefits of exercise.

* * *

A healthy self-esteem is fuel for courage and protects teen girls from the pressure to be perfect. Teens with a high self-esteem take care of themselves physically, mentally, and emotionally. They see themselves and others through a lens of acceptance and appreciation.

NURTURING AN AUTHENTIC SELF

A critical part of the teen years is finding out who you are and identifying what matters. It is a time to discover and harness personal strengths and values. Teens are notorious for testing the boundaries, trying on different identities, and exploring different interests, sports, and styles. All of these are important in order for them to discover their Authentic Self. However, in a world that also favors achievement and perfection, it is easy for them to lose sight of who they really are and what really matters.

Consider the differences between these beliefs:

> **BELIEF 1:**
> I'm a straight A-student.
> **BELIEF 2:**
> I choose to work hard because I care about doing my personal best and I enjoy the benefits.

> **BELIEF 1:**
> I am a bad kid. I'm always in trouble.
> **BELIEF 2:**
> I've made some mistakes and had to deal with the consequences, but I can make different choices and experience different outcomes.

When a teen has a strong sense of self and roots her identity in her inner qualities, her perspective of who she is will change. She will recognize that her wins and mistakes are a result of her choices, and her choices are largely determined by her values and how she thinks about herself.

WHO AM I?

Nikki is an only child and since elementary school, she has been labeled a star athlete and student. Outside of school, she spent her time studying or playing golf. When we met, her demeanor was serious and focused. She told me about school and golf. She admitted she did not have many close friends and did not do what "other girls my age do." She seemed eager for a connection and warmed quickly to me. She took her coaching sessions very seriously. In fact, she called her sessions "classes."

For her entire life, Nikki was praised for her good grades and precision in the game of golf. When I asked her, "What do your straight A's and golf handicap say about you?" Her answer was simple and direct, "That I'm a good student and decent golfer." "OK. What qualities make you a good student and decent golfer?" She was silent.

Nikki did not know a world outside of sports or straight A's. Although she had accomplished more than many 14-year-olds, she had a weak connection to the inner qualities and skills that led to her accomplishments.

Your teen's Authentic Self goes beyond her accomplishments. Her Authentic Self is a combination of her strengths, values, talents, and wisdom. But too often, teens (and adults) fall into the trap of defining themselves by their accomplishments only. While accomplishments are definitely a source of healthy pride, truly connecting to an Authentic Self requires connection to the aspects of self that led to an accomplishment. When your teen can identify, own, and celebrate these parts of herself, she can truly connect with her Authentic Self and allow it to shine!

 Name five accomplishments.

Think both big and small; remember that an accomplishment is anything that makes you feel good. Consider each and ask, what quality is reflected in this accomplishment? What skill, attitude, or mindset supported your teen in each accomplishment.

 Now, recall five recent challenges.

Invite your teen to consider how she got through these challenges. Again, identify the quality, skill, attitude, or mindset that helped her overcome the challenge and move forward. If some of the challenges are ongoing, ask which qualities, skills, attitudes, or mindsets would be helpful in supporting her through the challenge.

 **Take a personality assessment.**

My favorites are the VIA Strengths Finder or Enneagram. Both provide insight into personal qualities. Compare the findings with the qualities your daughter identified. Ask her which resonate with her. Encourage her to own them! Celebrate them! And allow them to transform her life.

* * *

Discovering and embracing an Authentic Self is a key to healthy self-esteem. A girl who is able to step fully into her Authentic Self is able to take ownership of her decisions and act in accordance with what is important to her.

UNCOVERING A PASSION

For some teens, their passion is obvious. They light up when playing their sport. They can't stop talking about a new technological discovery. They dedicate time to making art or playing an instrument. Some teens can even name their passions, but many others have not yet discovered what lights them up. They may go through high school bored and unengaged. These are the teens who need support, and a little extra coaching, to get on a path of passion and purpose.

Your teen's Spark* is what makes her light up. Sparks may be music, sports, writing poetry, helping friends, or working in the community. It is what fills her with excitement and enthusiasm. Sometimes Sparks can be bright and obvious, but sometimes they hide under fear or uncertainty. More often, the Spark needs to be discovered and ignited.

Here's how to help your teen to connect with her Spark:

 Tap into her skills or talents.

Does your daughter love to write, draw, sing, or dance? If there is something she is naturally good at and enjoys, this may be her Spark. Purposefully notice it and compliment her on her enthusiasm, skill, talent, or dedication.

ENTANGLED IN FEAR

Lauren slouched on the couch in my office. Her expression was sullen as she told me how her parents were "making" her sign up for an extra curricular class in which she had no interest. She was perfectly content going to school and playing video games or Snapchatting with friends when she got home. She saw no benefits to getting involved in a club or sport. On the contrary, she viewed any extra-curricular activity as a waste of time and money. "I mean, why would they want to spend all that money on something that I don't even care about?" She lamented. "I'm perfectly fine."

I sensed that Lauren's outward resistance to trying something new was coming from fear. Through various self-discovery practices, Lauren started to learn more about herself. She started to see how her tendencies to give up or take the easy way out, were not serving her well. She actually avoided trying anything new because she was afraid of failing, not being good enough, and being in the spotlight. After a few coaching sessions, she developed a new understanding of her fears. She realized they stemmed from fictitious stories she told herself about herself and her abilities. As she developed self-awareness and learned how to reframe her fears, she realized she did in fact have interests and passions. She loved animals! She wanted to learn more about the facilities where animals were used to help children with learning disabilities. She also was open to seeking volunteer opportunities at local animal shelters.

Notice if your teen is committed to a particular cause.

Is there a particular area that she cares deeply about? The environment? Animals? Friends? Help her get involved in charities or organizations that align with her passion.

 Observe what is unique about your teen's character.

Is there a part of her personality that stands out to you and others? Share your own uniqueness and help her discover the amazing qualities that make her who she is and then celebrate it!

 Rekindle your own Spark.

What were you like as a child? What did you love to do? What Sparks your life today? Share your Spark enthusiastically with your teen.

 Help her wonder about potential Sparks.

Any time you have a chance, ask her questions that get her thinking about her passions, dreams, and interests. Use these for starters: Have you ever wondered what it might be like to…? Imagine what it would feel like to…?

When your daughter connects with her Spark, be prepared to support it with encouragement and opportunity.

Seek out places and people who will foster her passion. Brace yourself for her newly found energy and excitement!

* * *

Helping your teen find her Spark and helping her nurture it are as important as buckling her seat belt or brushing her teeth. Why? Because it is the Spark that illuminates her path and purpose. When your teen recognizes her Spark and lets it shine brightly, she will be more content, satisfied, and motivated.

*Spark is a term coined by Dr. Peter Benson, founder of the Search Institute and a leading expert on adolescence.

THRIVING THROUGH CHANGE

The teen years are defined by change. Puberty is a time of marked physical changes as well as drastic shifts in attitude, energy, and mood. Aside from developmental changes, external changes such as parents' divorce, changing schools, or losing a beloved pet can derail a teen.

STARTING OVER

Elizabeth was 13 when she moved to California from the Midwest, and she was anything but thrilled. She missed her friends from home and said time and time again that she never wanted to move. "This was not my choice. My parents are torturing me! I don't even get along with people here." She spoke as if she had landed on another planet. Then she started to share her fears. Would she fit in? Would her teachers like her? Would she be able to keep up in school? Would her friends from home forget about her? Elizabeth clearly needed a place to vent, to process her anger and fear, and learn strategies for settling into a new school, making new friends, and starting again.

Change can often ignite fear in teenagers. Their minds focus on all the bad things that can happen. To help your teen thrive through change, consider the following.

> - Anticipate
> - Communicate
> - Encourage

#1 Anticipate.

Before a pending change, have an honest conversation about what your teen can expect. Ask what she is excited about and what worries her most. Honor her fears and worries, as unrealistic as they might be. Share the realities and facts. Ask her what support she will need. Make a support plan. Clearly state what you will do to make the transition easier and what resources she can tap into outside the home.

#2 Communicate.

As your teen begins a transition, make it a point to keep the lines of communication open. Do not expect that once you are adjusted, she has done the same. Set aside time for regular, gentle check-ins. Ask her if she would like to talk and then inquire about what has been easy and what remains challenging. On a daily basis, you can shift your questions from "How was your day?" and "How is it going?" to more specific open-ended questions like, "What was the best part of your day?" or "Would you tell me more about…?" If she does not open up easily, allow her time and space. Let her know you are there for her when she is ready to share.

#3 Encourage.

Adjusting to change is not easy. It can throw a teen's world into frenzy, causing stress to both you and her. Throughout a transition, stay attuned to your teen's attitude, energy, and mood. If you notice significant changes, consider ways to minimize stressors:

- Lighten up on her household chores.
- Streamline her schedule.
- Cut out one of her least favorite activities.

It is important for you to anticipate extreme reactions and cultivate your own balance, so you can provide calm, steady encouragement.

* * *

Change is the only thing we can count on so it is important to prepare your teen to respond to changes with trust and calm. Following the Anticipate, Communicate, Encourage model will invite your teen to see the bright side of change, learn to let go of the past, and embrace the future.

DEVELOPING LEADERSHIP SKILLS

More and more teens are stepping into the spotlight to share their experiences, demand action, and promote change. However, many teens avoid leadership because they fear being in an unwelcoming spotlight. When it comes to taking charge, some would argue that girls have a harder time. They face obstacles including being seen as petty, weak, or incapable. Girls will shy away from leadership opportunities when they feel they will be ridiculed or shamed for a mistake or mishap. They also steer away from leadership opportunities when they fear they will be seen as demanding and controlling. When a teen girl learns how to shift her perspective about leadership and step into her power with self-compassion and confidence, excitement lights her eyes. She will readily uncover opportunities to take the lead in performances, service organizations, at home, with friends, and in her classroom. The unwanted spotlight changes to a more welcomed spotlight, where she feels and shares the positive power of her leadership.

Being a leader means being able to make decisions with confidence and assurance. To do so, girls must first understand their personal values and how their values guide their actions. When this happens, a sense of integrity develops and it becomes easier to take on leadership roles.

TEEN LEADER: CHARLEY

Charley was a vibrant, friendly, and inspiring high-school senior. We met at a local volunteer event for foster youth, where she was one of the lead organizers. She was instrumental in getting several local business owners and at least a dozen high-school students to donate time and services for the event. Her strong passion for helping others was evident, as was her dedication to inspiring involvement in her peers and adults alike. In addition to helping foster youth, Charley volunteered for multiple local organizations. She led food drives, fundraising events, and took time to care for furry friends at local shelters. At school, Charley started two popular clubs, one for peer mentors and one for helping underserved youth. Charley did not let fear of failure or self-doubt get in the way of her passion for helping others and leading others to do the same.

If your daughter has untapped leadership potential, use these ideas and questions to inspire a thoughtful dialogue and encourage her to step confidently into leadership roles:

#1 You are the choices that you make.

Ask: How is this true for you?

#2 Paradigms are perceptions, how you see things, people, and experiences.

Ask: How do your perceptions shape your choices?

#3 Habits are powerful and important.

Ask: How do your habits impact your life at school? With friends? In sports?

#4 Values inform your choices.

Ask: What are your values? What values-based choices have you made?

* * *

During the teen years, leadership can manifest in many different ways. As parents, teachers, and coaches, we can help teens develop habits and values that create a strong foundation for leadership.

PUTTING IT ALL TOGETHER

What do you now understand about your teen's personal growth?

_____
_____
_____
_____
_____
_____
_____
_____
_____
_____
_____
_____
_____
_____
_____
_____
_____
_____
_____
_____
_____
_____
_____
_____
_____

How will you begin to parent differently?

- Make sure to share you newly found knowledge!

SECTION FIVE:

TOOLS FOR LIFE

RESPONSIBILITY

Teen responsibility comes in many forms: homework, time management, household chores, driving, observing curfews, and social decision-making. When homework goes missing, chores are skipped, curfew is ignored, and harmful actions are repeated with little sign of remorse or awareness, parents rightfully get concerned.

WITH RESPONSIBILITY COMES FREEDOM

Nicole's parents had reason to worry. They set clear expectations for homework, upheld a reasonable curfew, and provided an allowance on the condition that the weekly laundry was folded and nightly dinner dishes were washed. Time and time again, Nicole would turn in assignments late or not at all. She broke curfew and rarely completed her weekly chores. She had very little sense of responsibility and very little understanding of why these things were important. When she came to see me, she explained that her parents were so controlling. "They don't allow me to do anything and they ask me to do way too much around the house!"

There was an obvious disconnect. Nicole needed to understand why being responsible is important. She also needed to make the connection between responsibility and freedom, something she strongly desired. Through coaching, Nicole began to see her parents' "rules" in a different way. Slowly, she began to understand that in order to get what she wanted, she needed to demonstrate maturity and trust, by following through on the minimal expectations set by her parents.

Teaching your teen how to be responsible can be a frustrating task. If your efforts are leading to anger, arguments, and even more complacency on the part of your teen, it is time to try something new.

 Reframe your message.

Instead of telling her what she needs to do and when, try making a request. This simple shift demonstrates a level of respect that she will respond to better than a parental demand. Allow a conversation to unfold that empowers her and helps her feel ownership over the task. When she feels respected, she is much more likely to act responsibly.

 Help her get organized.

Sometimes a teen's resistance is code that she needs support. Try asking her if she knows how to do what is expected and help her get started. Show her how to set reminders on her phone, efficiently complete household chores, approach her huge stack of homework, organize her backpack and binder, etc. This does not mean doing it for her, but teaching her how to do it for herself.

 Notice and praise.

This goes back to the old saying, "catch 'em being good." Pay attention and acknowledge when you see her being responsible. Avoid the "I told you so" approach and, instead, offer her praise for taking action, being helpful, independent, and organized.

Teach her that life is a series of choices.

Understanding the impact of choices is key to becoming more responsible. Teens are naturally impulsive and often learn the hard way that their actions have consequences. You can foster an understanding that life is a series of choices and certain choices have certain outcomes. Use the word "choice" as you involve her in decision making. Share your own decision-making process, highlighting the choices you make and the outcomes of those choices. This will help your teen build the bridge between actions and consequences.

* * *

Responsibility develops over time, so patience and persistence are key. If you practice making requests rather than demands, the tension around getting things done will subside. When you ask if she knows how to do what you are asking, you will be able to recognize what support is needed. As your teen gains a sense of responsibility, allow her more freedom and continue to praise responsible action.

GRIT AND RESILIENCE

Almost every teen I meet has faced discouraging life events: bad grades, social rejection, losing a loved one, or dealing with absent or abusive parents. Depending on the teen, these challenges can trigger a stream of negative self-talk, fear, doubt, or even thoughts of giving up.

SHATTERED

At the age of 15, Kelly had already lost her best friend, moved to a new city, and dealt with her parents' contentious divorce. She was subdued, spoke softly, and held her body tightly. She told me her mom, who was the head of her primary home, worried about her and thought she spent too much time alone. Her mom did not like the horror films and novels she was interested in watching. She told me reading was her way of escaping. She felt isolated in her new school and while she did not talk much about her parents' separation, I could tell she felt plagued by guilt. She preferred to live at her mom's house because it was "easier" but she felt she let her dad down. When I asked Kelly what was good about starting in a new town and having an opportunity to meet new friends, she shrugged. She was pretty sure she would always be miserable and she was never going to meet another best friend.

Grit is the ability to use courage and strength to get through challenging situations. Resilience is the ability to bounce back from a setback. Both help make it easier to handle challenges and can prevent negative emotions from getting in the way.

Take a moment to consider how your teen handles setbacks. Does she retreat, sulk, or fall into a depression? Does she talk things through, look for solutions, and take action? Does she view setbacks and challenges as opportunities to learn, grow, and change? Imagine if your daughter could handle life's challenges without being overwhelmed. What would be different if she actually embraced the challenges, knowing that on the other side, she would find greater strength?

The following practices will promote grit and resilience.

 Foster relationships with people outside the family.

At birth, your child develops a sense of safety and security through her family relationships. During elementary school, middle school, and high school, her relationships with adults expand to teachers, coaches, and members of the community. These connections are key to providing teens with a sense of identity and belonging. This network serves as your teen's trusty support system. When she knows there are adults, other than her parents, whom she can turn to for information or advice, she will feel more capable and supported, especially through a challenge.

Build on your teen's personal strengths and values.

Make a list of the qualities (not achievements) that make your teen unique. Start to verbally honor these traits using the words "respect" and "admire." This will help your teen develop a strong sense of self and positive self-esteem. She will begin to see herself as a person who embodies these qualities. These positive beliefs in herself will make it easier for her to overcome challenges and bounce back from adversity.

 Provide experiences that encourage autonomy and responsibility.

Allow your teen to do age-appropriate things independently and accept the natural consequences of her choices. These experiences will ultimately teach her an important skill-set for solving problems on her own.

* * *

Grit and resilience help your teen know and trust that she can handle the ups and downs of life. With this understanding, she is more likely to be happy, motivated, and proactive.

COMPASSION AND GRATITUDE

In this increasingly competitive world, it can be hard for teens to truly feel good about themselves or their accomplishments. Everywhere they turn, there is an opportunity to self-evaluate or compare. Too often, this triggers a cycle of "I'm not enough…" messages:

- I'm not smart enough.
- I'm not athletic enough.
- I'm not good looking enough.

These beliefs are devastating to a teen's self-esteem. They increase the negative cycles of comparison, perpetuate self-doubt, and make it almost impossible for them to find the good in anything.

PLAGUED BY SELF-DOUBT

At 16, Juliann was struggling. She constantly told herself she was not good enough and consequently, she refused to try a new sport or activity. She was frozen with a fear of failure and letting others down. Although she was doing well in school, she complained about her teachers. "They don't like me," she would insist. She had a few good friends, but said, "They're more into each other than me. That's fine. I'm not as exciting as the others." Besides coming to her weekly coaching sessions and going to school, she preferred to spend her time engrossed in a sci-fi book or binge-watching Netflix.

In my coaching practice, I spend a lot of time helping girls understand their "Negative Nag" or Gremlin. This is an inner voice that can seize their personal power and convince them that the lie of "not good enoughness" is true. It can also spin complicated and unsubstantiated imaginings about worst-case scenarios or what others think. This inner voice is powerful and can paralyze teens with doubt, worry, or fear. But when they learn to minimize its power by replacing its unkind and unhelpful messages with those that are energizing, compassionate and truthful, everything changes. These are messages of gratitude and they are exactly what turns down the volume of the "Negative Nag" or Gremlin. Study after study proves that increasing gratitude paves a way to positive emotions and self-compassion. When girls turn up the volume of gratitude, their anxiety lowers, and focus and energy increase. Moreover, when your daughter feels good about herself, she is able to see the good in others.

Talk about self-compassion.

Self-compassion is not a term commonly used by teens, but it is an important tool. I define self-compassion as feeling good by respecting your whole self, including your strengths and your weaknesses. It is about being your own best friend, taking care of yourself, honoring your emotions, and recognizing the temporary nature of challenging feelings and situations. Practicing self-compassion leads to increased confidence and happiness, and an ability to handle the "tough stuff" without getting derailed.

#2 Make gratitude a family practice.

Share a daily gratitude over the dinner table or have a family gratitude journal. If you have a crafty teen, make a family gratitude jar. Transform an ordinary mason jar into a container for your gratitude and appreciation. Decorate the jar with inspirational phrases, symbols and pictures that represent gratitude. Place the jar in a common area in your home, along with a stack of mini Post-it® Notes. Each day, write something you are grateful for on a Post-it® Note and place it in the jar. The jar is also an effective visual reminder to be grateful.

#3 Maximize technology.

Capitalize on social media and texting to inspire compassion and gratitude. Teens notoriously share on social media, so why not turn these posts into opportunities for fostering compassion? Encourage your teen to be empathetic when responding to an angry message; suggest she consider what it must be like to be the aggressor. How does she think it would be different if the aggressor were sharing this message in person? Would her face-to-face response be different from a post?

Use texting to foster gratitude. Send a daily gratitude to your teen. You will be surprised how fun and easy it is and it will inspire your teen to see the good in life. Perhaps she will extend the practice, texting positive messages to her friends.

#4 Nix the Negative Nag.

When your teen starts to express the comments of the Negative Nag, ask how those thoughts could be replaced with something more productive. Inquire with open-ended questions like, "How can you turn that around?" or "If you chose not to listen to the messages of the Negative Nag, what other message would you hear?" This encourages out-of-the-box thinking and uncovers more helpful ways responding.

* * *

Compassion and gratitude are attitudes that support your teen's ability to relate to themselves, others, and their world with kindness and empathy. They enable her to find the opportunities in challenges and shield her from self-judgement. Compassion and gratitude propel her forward with a resilient heart and open mind. They truly are two essential life-skills.

PUTTING IT ALL TOGETHER

What do you now understand about tools for life?

How will you begin to parent differently?

_____

- Make sure to share you newly found knowledge!

BRINGING IT ALL TOGETHER

CONCLUSION

Parenting teens requires patience, trust, support, and a new set of tools! As you move forward on your parenting journey, there will be bumps in the road. There will be new trends and unforeseeable challenges. When you feel unable to keep up, remember what you really want for your teen and yourself. Pause, refocus, and find ways to support yourself. Take a break and a few deep breaths. Trust that you can find an effective response to even the most heartbreaking or earth-shattering situations. Remember what really matters: sustaining a strong bond with your teen and supporting her toward happy, healthy, and responsible independence.

This book is your go-to-guide, but if you would like more personalized support, I can help.

My website includes helpful resources and parenting suggestions. From here, you can also subscribe to my monthly newsletter, where I share parenting tips and upcoming events.

My personalized parent-coaching programs address your specific concerns and provide support, insight, and valuable information related to raising your teen.

My teen and young adult coaching focuses on specific objectives and promotes your daughter's self-awareness, confidence, and action toward positive change.

Visit my website:
https://www.inspirebalance.com

Follow me on:
Facebook:
https://www.facebook.com/Erica.InspireBalanceCoaching/

Instagram:
https://www.instagram.com/erica_inspire_balance/

LinkedIn:
https://www.linkedin.com/in/erica-rood/

4114U

TOOLS FOR TEENS

TOOLS FOR TEENS ACTIVITIES

This section contains some of my favorite tools for teens. There are suggestions for how parents can present the tools and/or use them alongside their teen, as a way to stay connected and start important conversations.

Circle of Friends 109

For Teens: Who are your friends? Why are they your friends? In the heart-shape, write the names of your Best Friends. Outside the heart, write the names of your Good Friends, Pretty Good Friends, Hi-Bye Friends, and finally, your Frenemies. As you write their names, think about the qualities of each person. Are they kind, honest, loyal, or helpful?

For Parents: Use this tool to help your teen develop an understanding of friendships. Talk about different types of friends: Best Friends, Good Friends, Pretty Good Friends, Hi-Bye Friends, and Frenemies. Ask about the people who are in each category and follow up with a discussion about the qualities that define each type of friend. For example, a Best Friend might be loyal, honest, reliable, etc.

Consider the Possibilities 111

For Teens: This is a simple way to expand your perspective of a situation and get out of your head. When you can identify alternative perspectives and possibilities, you will be able to handle challenging situations with clarity and mind-strength.

For Parents: Too often teens have tunnel vision and can not see beyond their own feelings or perspective. Use the questions in this tool to help your teen gain a broader perspective and different point of view.

Empathy Pro 112

For Teens: Empathy strengthens relationships and improves communication. Use this tool to better understand someone else and practice empathy.

For Parents: Use the questions in this tool to inspire a deep conversation about empathy and its importance.

Flipping the Switch 113

For Teens: Do not let thoughts of self-doubt or negativity get in your way. Use this tool to flip the switch and turn heavy, negative thoughts into more uplifting, positive thoughts.

For Parents: Do this alongside your teen. Show her that you too have negative or doubtful thoughts and you have to practice turning them around so they do not stop you from moving forward or make you feel badly about yourself. Model your humility and honesty.

Goals for the Year 114

For Teens: You can use this tool when you start a new school year, calendar year, or birth year. The goal is to get clear and intentional about what you want in each category of your life. Take a moment to think about what you really want for yourself. Dream big, see the goals becoming a reality, and when you write them down, be as specific as possible.

For Parents: Use this tool alongside your teen. Set your own goals. Talk about how you can support each other in achieving your goals, what small steps you will take to get started, and what personal qualities will help you achieve your goals.

Gratitude Bingo/Gratitude Prompts 115

For Teens: Gratitude fosters feelings of accomplishment and joy. Use this to inspire journal entries or spark conversations with friends and family.

For Parents: Start a conversation about the importance and power of gratitude. Use this tool to inspire a conversation about gratitude or play a creative game.

Is It Really What You Think It Is? 116

For Teens: Do you find yourself jumping to conclusions and making up stories about certain people or situations? When this happens, you may overreact or respond to a person or situation in a way that makes things worse. Use this tool to unpack some of those stories or beliefs so you can speak your truth and feel better!

For Parents: Use this tool alongside your teen. Talk about how your misunderstandings have steered you wrong or caused you to react to presumptions rather than truth. Start a conversation about why it is important to pause and examine initial beliefs about a situation or person so you can see the truth and respond in an authentic way.

Let It Go Letter 117

For Teens: Use this letter to process difficult feelings and thoughts. As you write, consider "emptying" your heart and mind. Be completely raw and honest. Say all that you need and want to say. Writing this letter to a person or situation that has caused you pain will help you let go of hard feelings and move on.

For Parents: Provide this letter as a framework for your daughter to write or talk about difficult feelings.

-103-

Invite her to share it with you or allow her to keep it private. Encourage her to do the process as many times as needed in order to feel fully released of the burdensome feelings or memories.

LP3 or List, Prune, Prioritize, and Plan 119

For Teens: Life can get overwhelming, especially when you have one of those weeks where homework, projects, and tests pile up in the same week. Use this tool to get a handle on your to-dos and create a strategy for tackling what you need to do without getting stressed and overwhelmed. Trust me, it works.

For Parents: Introduce this process to your teen and model practicing it yourself. You can talk through the process but it is much more effective to write things out. Your teen may also need your support in creating a plan. When doing so, keep in mind that your system for organizing your to-dos may or may not be effective for your teen. Keep an open mind and introduce multiple ways to organize time and projects.

Plan for Restoring Peace 121

For Teens: After a fight with a friend, boyfriend, or parent, it can be hard to know whether or not to move on or make amends. Use this tool to clear your head and determine your best next steps.

For Parents: Use the language in this tool to talk with your teen about how to handle conflict and restore peace.

Power Up Your Journaling 122

For Teens: Journaling is one of the most effective and simple ways to shift your mood and process feelings. It can also be really hard to know where to start. Use these journal prompts to inspire one sentence each day, or even more.

For Parents: Sharing a journal with your teen can offer a sacred and special place for meaningful conversations. The journal prompts on this page can help you and your teen get started.

Responsibility Wheel 123

For Teens: What is the best part of being more responsible? More freedom! When you want to increase your level of responsibility, start with this "snapshot." Think about how responsible you are in each area of your life. Give each area a score. A zero would be not at all responsible, whereas a 10 would be totally responsible. In the areas where you see a middle or low score, ask yourself: How can I be more responsible in that part of my life?

For Parents: Start a conversation about responsibilities. Use the wheel to talk about actions that demonstrate responsibility in each area. The wheel can also inspire a dialogue about expectations, support, and consequences.

Sometimes I Wish I Could 124

For Teens: When you are feeling discouraged or lost, use this tool to dream, generate ideas, and find clarity. You may uncover a new passion or be able to determine a helpful action for change.

For Parents: Reframe the statements on this page into open-ended questions to start an inspiring and eye-opening conversation about what is possible. Ask your teen what support she might need to get into action and change "I wish..." to "I will..."

Strengths and Behavior Clarification.................125

For Teens: What are your top five strengths? On the page, write your top strengths and then for each, write a behavior that matches. For example, if one of your strengths is gratitude, a matching behavior could be keeping a gratitude journal.

For Parents: Use this tool alongside your teen. Talk about your own strengths and how they have guided you in your life. Start a conversation about the strengths that you each still want to develop and how you might do that.

What's Behind Your Goals? A Guide to Uncovering Your Why..126

For Teens: Getting connected to your "why" can help you stay motivated to take the action required to achieve your goals. Use this simple process to uncover what's behind your goal and clarify your "why."

For Parents: Use this simple process with your teen. You can work through the page together or simply use the questions to help your teen get clear and connected to her "why."

What's in a Friend? 127

For Teens: When talking about what really matters to you in a friend, it can be hard to find the words. Most teens say they appreciate their friends for being "nice" or "fun," but in truth, strong friendships go way beyond kindness and fun. Use this list to get crystal clear about what you value and cherish in your friends and what you are hoping to find in future friends.

For Parents: When you are helping your teen navigate the ups and downs of a friendship, you can use this list of qualities to spark meaningful discussions about what your daughter is looking for in a friend and which qualities have been violated by a friend. You can also present this list and talk about what each quality means and why they are important in a friendship.

Who Are You? 129

For Teens: What qualities make you unique? This is a fun, simple way to get clear on who you are and what you stand for. Read the words on each list and highlight your top five-ten in each category.

For Parents: Use this tool alongside your teen. Highlight your own strengths, values, talents, and interests. Talk about how they have changed and developed over time and through life experiences. Share what strengths, values, talents, and interests you see in each other and why.

4114U

Circle of Friends Activity

For Teens:

- Who are your friends?
- Why are they your friends?

In the heart-shape, write the names of your Best Friends. Outside the heart, write the names of your Good Friends, Pretty Good Friends, Hi-Bye Friends, and finally, your Frenemies. As you write their names, think about the qualities of each person. Are they kind, honest, loyal, or helpful?

For Parents:

- Use this tool to help your teen develop an understanding of friendships.

- Talk about different types of friends:
    - Best Friends
    - Good Friends
    - Pretty Good Friends
    - Hi-Bye Friends
    - Frenemies.

Ask about the people who are in each category and follow up with a discussion about the qualities that define each type of friend. For example, a Best Friend might be loyal, honest, reliable, etc.

Circle of Friends Activity

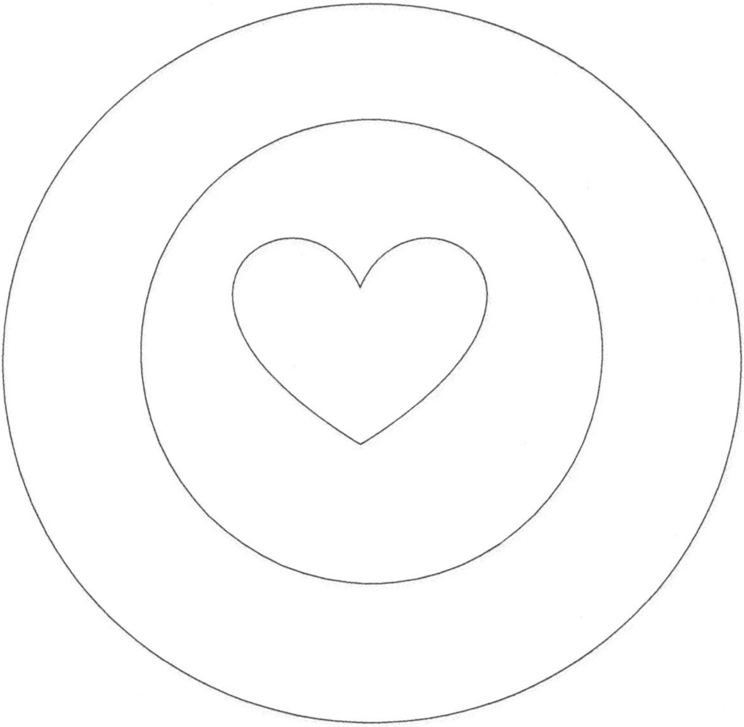

Consider the Possibilities

FOR TEENS:
This is a simple way to expand your perspective of a situation and get out of your own head. When you can identify alternative perspectives and possibilities, you will be able to handle challenging situations with clarity and mind-strength.

FOR PARENTS:
Too often teens have tunnel vision and can't see beyond their own feelings or perspective. Use the questions in this tool to help your teen gain a broader perspective and different point of view.

Consider the Possibilities

Try coming up with some new reasons why people do what they do.

What happened?	Your interpretation?	What else could be going on?

Empathy Pro

FOR TEENS:
Empathy strengthens relationships and improves communication. Use this tool to better understand someone else and practice empathy.

FOR PARENTS:
Use the questions in this tool to inspire a deep conversation about empathy and its importance.

Empathy Pro

Empathy means being able to understand how someone else feels and then treat people accordingly. Practicing empathy requires a type of mind-trick. You have to direct your mind to a place it does not go to on its own. You have to step into someone else's world and then return to your own. How do you do this? Try this:

On whom do you want to practice your empathy mind-trick?

_____

What is their reality like?	What makes them feel happy?
What are their wants?	What are their needs?

Flipping the Switch

FOR TEENS:
Do not let thoughts of self-doubt or negativity get in your way. Use this tool to flip the switch and turn heavy, negative thoughts into more uplifting thoughts. This tool will help you feel energized and motivated.

FOR PARENTS:
Do this alongside your teen. Show her that you too have negative or doubtful thoughts and you have to practice turning them around so they do not stop you from moving forward or make you feel bad about yourself. Model your humility and honesty.

It is easy to get caught in a negative web of thoughts or feelings, especially when facing a challenge. The word labels we use to describe our experiences have a huge influence on the way we deal with those experiences. If we change the label, we can actually change our feelings and experiences.

Flipping the Switch	
My common negative thoughts or feelings?	**How can I flip them to more uplifting thoughts and feelings?**

Goals for the Year

FOR TEENS:
You can use this tool when you start a new school year, calendar year, or birth year. The goal is to get clear and intentional about what you want for yourself in each category of your life. Take a moment to think about what you really want for yourself. Dream big, to see your goals become a reality, and when you write them down, be as specific as possible.

FOR PARENTS:
Use this tool alongside your teen. Set your own goals. Talk about how you can support each other to achieve your goals, what small steps to take to get started, and what personal qualities will help you achieve your goals.

Goals for the Year

Academic Goals:
_____
_____

Friendship/Social Goals:
_____
_____

Family/Relationship Goals:
_____
_____

Athletic Goals:
_____
_____

Artistic/Creative Goals:
_____
_____

Personal Goals:
_____
_____

Essential Questions: How will you achieve your goals? What support do you require? What actions can you take today? What personal qualities will help you achieve your goals?

Gratitude Bingo/Gratitude Prompts

FOR TEENS:
Gratitude fosters feelings of accomplishment and joy. Use this to inspire journal entries or conversations with friends and family.

FOR PARENTS:
Start a conversation about the importance and power of gratitude. Use this tool to inspire a conversation about gratitude or play a creative game.

Gratitude Bingo/Gratitude Prompts

I am grateful for these things that I see...	I am grateful for these things that I hear...	I am grateful for these things that I smell...	I am grateful for these things that I feel...	I am grateful for these things that I taste...
I am grateful for these animals...	I am grateful for these friends...	I am grateful for these family members...	I am grateful for these teachers...	I am grateful for these things in my home...
I am grateful for the experience of...	I am grateful for my ability to...	I am grateful for my focus on...	I am grateful for this part of my personality...	I am grateful for this part of my body...
I am grateful for this challenge because it taught me...	I am grateful that I now understand...	I am grateful that I am capable of...	I am grateful that I can help others in this way...	I am grateful for my...
I appreciate myself for...	I am grateful that I accomplished...	I am grateful for this person in my life...	I am grateful for this part of nature...	I am grateful for this part of my community...

Is It Really What You Think It Is?

FOR TEENS:
Do you find yourself jumping to conclusions and making up stories about certain people or situations? When this happens, you may overreact or respond to a person or situation in way that makes things worse. Use this tool to unpack some of those stories or beliefs so you can speak your truth and feel better.

FOR PARENTS:
Use this tool alongside your teen. Talk about how your misunderstandings have steered you wrong or caused you to react to presumptions rather than truth. Start a conversation about why it is important to pause and examine initial beliefs about a situation or person so you can see the truth and respond in an authentic way.

Is it Really What You Think It Is?

What bad event or problem are you facing?	What thoughts or beliefs are triggered by this problem?	How does this thought or belief make you feel?	Go back to column one. What are other possible reasons this is happening?	What is a more optimistic or energizing belief that will help you feel happier and more hopeful?
My best friend hasn't called me in three days.	I believe she must not like me. Maybe she thinks I'm boring or annoying.	I feel lonely and confused. I feel like I'm not very good at keeping friends.	Maybe she's been really busy. Maybe she's going through something personal or needs time alone.	I am a good friend. I haven't done anything wrong. I am caring and fun. This is not about me.

Let-It-Go Letter

FOR TEENS:
Use this letter to process difficult feelings and thoughts. As you write, consider "emptying" your heart and mind. Be completely raw and honest. Say all that you need and want to say. Writing this letter to a person or situation that has caused you pain will help you let go of hard feelings and move on.

FOR PARENTS:
Provide this letter as a framework for your daughter to write or talk about difficult feelings. Invite her to share it with you or allow her to keep it private. Encourage her to do the process as many times as needed in order to feel fully released of burdensome feelings or memories.

A Let-It-Go Letter

Dear_____,

I am writing this letter so I can let go and move on.

What makes me angry is...
_____
_____

I am surprised by/that...
_____
_____

What hurts me most is...
_____
_____

I am disappointed in/that...
_____
_____

What I wish is...
_____
_____

Where I went wrong is...
_____
_____

What I am sorry about is...
_____
_____

What I really want you to know is...
_____
_____

What I now know is...
_____
_____

Something I have learned about myself is...
_____
_____

Something I have learned about you is...
_____
_____

What I want for myself now is...
_____
_____

LP3 Activity
List, Prune, Prioritize, and Plan

FOR TEENS:
Life can get overwhelming, especially when you have one of those weeks when homework, projects, and tests pile up in the same week. Use this tool to get a handle on your to-dos and create a strategy for tackling what you need to do without getting stressed and overwhelmed. Trust me, it works.

FOR PARENTS:
Introduce this process to your teen and model practicing it yourself. You can talk through the process but it's much more effective to write things out. Your teen may also need your support in creating a plan. When doing so, keep in mind that your system for organizing your to-dos may or may not be effective for your teen. Keep an open mind and introduce multiple ways to organize time and projects.

LP3 - List, Prune, Prioritize, and Plan

Step One: List
Make a list of all of your to-dos. Include everything that is on your mind now (and what wakes you up in the middle of the night.)

Step Two: Prune
Scrutinize your list. What is on your list that can be eliminated? What did you think you needed to do, but when you see it on your list, you know you do not need to accomplish it immediately?

Step Three: Prioritize
Re-order your list. Now that you have eliminated some items, prioritize what needs to get done right away, followed by what can wait, and what really does not need your attention for a few more weeks.

Step Four: Plan
Create a plan. Get out your calendar and decide when you will spend time on each of your to-dos. Allot a certain amount of time for each item.

Plan for Restoring Peace

FOR TEENS:
After a fight with a friend, boyfriend, or parent, it can be hard to know whether to move on or make amends. Use this tool to clear your head and determine your best next steps.

FOR PARENTS:
Use the language in this tool to talk with your teen about how to handle conflict and restore peace.

My Plan For Restoring Peace

How did my action hurt people?
_____
_____
_____

How did the hurting action decrease respect and trust that people have in me?
_____
_____
_____

What are three things I could have done instead of the hurting act?
_____
_____
_____

What are three ways I can earn back people's trust and respect over the next week?
_____
_____
_____

What amends do I need to make and to whom?
_____
_____
_____

How will people know I have kept my plan for restoring peace?
_____
_____
_____

Power Up Your Journaling

FOR TEENS:

Journaling is one of the most effective and simple ways to shift your mood and process feelings. It can also be really hard to know where to start. Use these journal prompts to inspire one sentence each day, or even more.

FOR PARENTS:

Sharing a journal with your teen can offer a sacred and special place for meaningful conversations. The journal prompts on this page can help you and your teen get started.

Journaling is one of the most effective and simple ways to shift your mood and process your feelings. If you have trouble getting started, use these prompts:

Get Journaling!	
• Something I did well today...	• I think my future is...
• I felt proud when...	• I gain strength from...
• Today I accomplished...	• I would never...
• I had a positive experience with...	• I was really happy when...
• Something I did for someone...	• I love when...
• I felt good about myself when...	• I struggle when...
• I was proud of someone else...	• I believe that...
• Today was interesting because...	• I get angry when...
• Sometimes I wish I could...	• I hope that...
• The thing I fear most is...	• I thrive when...
• Today I would like to...	• Today I would like to...
• I would really enjoy...	• I don't like to admit...
	• Today I believed that...

Responsibility Wheel

FOR TEENS:
What is the best part of being more responsible? More freedom. When you want to increase your level of responsibility, start with this "snapshot." Think about how responsible you are in each area of your life. Give each area a score. A zero would be not at all responsible, whereas a 10 would be totally responsible. In the areas where you see a middle or low score, ask yourself: How can I be more responsible in that part of my life?

FOR PARENTS:
Start a conversation about responsibilities. Use the wheel to talk about actions that demonstrate responsibility in each area. The wheel can also inspire a dialogue about expectations, support, and consequences.

Responsibility Wheel
Responsibility means having the opportunity to make decisions and act independently. Use the Responsibility Wheel to rate your level of responsibility in each area of your life. After rating, describe specific responsibilities in each area (i.e. What needs to be done? Who needs to do it? Why it needs to be done?) Then consider, what are the consequences when you do not meet each responsibility? How do those consequences effect you? Can you make changes? Do you need to?

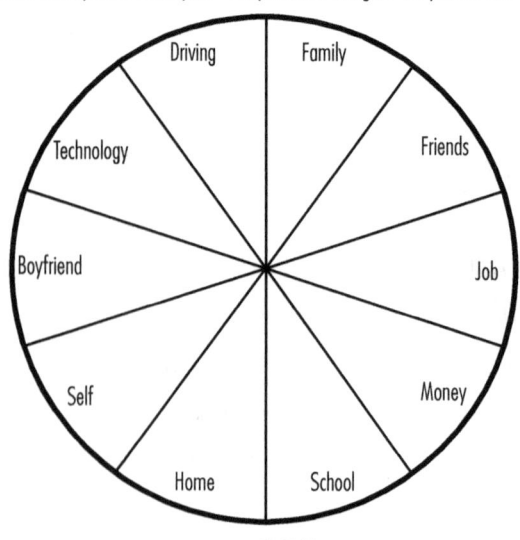

Sometimes I Wish I Could

FOR TEENS:
When you are feeling discouraged or lost, use this tool to dream, generate ideas and find clarity. You may uncover a new passion or determine a helpful action for change.

FOR PARENTS:
Reframe the statements on this page into open-ended questions to start an inspiring and eye-opening conversation about what is possible. Ask your teen what support she might need to get into action and change "I wish I could" to "I will..." statements.

Sometimes I Wish I Could...

Sometimes I wish I could...

The thing I fear most is...

Today I would like to...

I feel my future is...

I gain strength from...

I was really happy when...

I love when...

I struggle when...

I believe that...

Today I fear that...

I hope that..

I secretly enjoy...

I would like to...

Strengths –> Behavior Clarification

FOR PARENTS:

Use this tool alongside your teen. Talk about your own strengths and how they have guided you in your life. Also share what strengths you both want to develop and how to do that.

STRENGTHS	BEHAVIOR
• Appreciation of beauty & excellence • Bravery • Creativity • Curiosity • Fairness • Forgiveness • Gratitude • Honesty • Humility • Intellectual curiosity • Judgment • Kindness • Leadership • Perseverance • Perspective • Prudence • Social Intelligence • Self-Regulation • Sense of Humor • Team player • Zest Any others?	

What's Behind Your Goals?
A Guide to Uncovering Your Why

FOR TEENS:
Getting connected to your "why" can help you stay motivated to take the action required to achieve your goals. Use this simple process to uncover what is behind your goals and clarify your "why."

FOR PARENTS:
Use this simple process with your teen. You can work through the page together or simply use the questions to help your teen get clear and connected to her "why."

What's Behind Your Goals?
A guide to uncovering your WHY.

What is one goal or outcome you would like to experience?
_____
_____

Why do you want this? How will achieving this goal or outcome impact you?
_____
_____

Why do you want that experience? What is important about having that experience?
_____
_____

Why is that important?
_____
_____

And, why is that important?
_____
_____

What will achieving this goal mean for you? How will you feel? How will you change?
_____
_____

THIS IS YOUR WHY.

What's in a Friend?

FOR TEENS:
When talking about what really matters to you in a friend, it can be hard to find the words. Most teens say they appreciate their friends for being "nice" or "fun", but in truth, strong friendships go way beyond kindness and fun. Use this list to get crystal clear about what you value and cherish in your friends and what you are hoping to find in future friends.

FOR PARENTS:
When you are helping your teen navigate the ups and downs of a friendship, you can use this list of qualities to spark meaningful discussions about what your daughter is looking for in a friend and which qualities have been violated by a friend. You can also present this list and talk about what each quality means and why it is important in a friendship.

What's in a Friend? Activity

1. Accountability
2. Adventure
3. Authenticity
4. Balance
5. Beauty
6. Boldness
7. Calmness
8. Collaboration
9. Compassion
10. Comradeship
11. Confidence
12. Connectedness
13. Contentment
14. Cooperation
15. Courage
16. Creativity
17. Curiosity
18. Determination
19. Directness
20. Ease
21. Effortlessness
22. Enthusiasm
23. Fairness
24. Flexibility
25. Focus
26. Forgiveness
27. Freedom
28. Fun
29. Generosity
30. Gentleness
31. Happiness
32. Harmony
33. Helpfulness
34. Honesty
35. Humor
36. Independence
37. Integrity
38. Intuition
39. Joy
40. Kindness
41. Learning
42. Listening
43. Love
44. Loyalty
45. Optimism
46. Participation
47. Partnership
48. Passion
49. Patience
50. Peace
51. Presence
52. Recognition
53. Respect
54. Resourcefulness
55. Safety
56. Self-esteem
57. Simplicity
58. Spontaneity
59. Strength
60. Thankfulness
61. Tolerance
62. Trust
63. Understanding
64. Wisdom
65. _____
66. _____
67. _____
68. _____
69. _____
70. _____
71. _____
72. _____
73. _____
74. _____
75. _____
76. _____

Who Are You?

FOR TEENS:

What qualities make you unique? This is a fun, simple way to get clear on who you are and what you stand for. Read the words on each list and highlight your top five-ten in each category.

FOR PARENTS:

Use this tool alongside your teen. Highlight your own strengths, values, talents, and interests. Talk about how they have changed and developed over time and through life experiences. Share what strengths, values, talents, and interests you see in each other and why.

Who Are You? Activity

Strengths - What are your strongest attributes and qualities?
Values - What is important to you? What do you care about?
Talents - What do you really enjoy, are good at, and/or improving?
Interests - What things are you interested in or what would you like to learn more about?

STRENGTHS	VALUES	TALENTS	INTERESTS
Analytical	Adventure	Art	Animals
Artistic ability	Beauty	Baking	Art
Athleticism	Communication	Building	Cultures
Cheerfulness	Competition	Computers	Dating
Cooperation	Discipline	Cooking	Design
Creativity	Fairness	Design	Exploring
Determination	Family	Helping	Fashion
Energetic	Fitness	Humor	Future
Friendliness	Flexibility	Math	Helping
Helpfulness	Friendship	Music	Hiking
Intelligence	Fun	Photography	History
Leadership ability	Hard work	Reading	Music
Music	Honesty	Speaking	Nature
Open-mindedness	Humor	Sports	Performing
Organization	Independence	Teaching	Pets
Patience	Individuality	Writing	Politics
Personality	Kindness		Sports
Playfulness	Love		Teaching
Positivity	Peace		Technology
Responsibility	Playfulness		Travel
Sense of Humor	Relaxation		
Sense of Style	Vacations		
Thinker			
Trustworthiness			
Any others?	Any others?	Any others?	Any others?

QUESTIONS FOR CONTEMPLATION

Use these question for yourself or to inspire a group discussion.

GETTING STARTED

- When you think of your own teen years, what do you recall?
- What kind of support did you need? What kind of support did you appreciate?
- How did you view your parents?
- What do you think your parents could have done differently?
- What parallels do you see between your teen relationship with your parents and your teen's relationship with you?
- What has been the hardest part of your parenting journey?
- What has been the most cherished part of your parenting journey?

STAYING CONNECTED

- What does being connected to your teen mean? What does it look like?
- Do you feel connected to your teen? Why or why not?
- Can you relate to the description of Angela? In what ways?
- In what situations do you find it easy to ask open-ended questions and listen without judgment or problem-solving?
- Where can you set clearer or more consistent boundaries?
- How do you think your teen knows you respect her?
- In what ways do you show your teen respect?
- In what ways do they show you respect?
- When it comes to you and your teen, what are the key ingredients to staying connected?

SOCIAL WORLD

- What has been (or what do you think will be) the hardest part of parenting a teen through "Friend Drama?"
- What are some ways you have monitored social media and curtailed cyberbullying?
- How do you teach your teen to be respectfully assertive?
- How is empathy encouraged in your family?
- How do you view popularity? How do you view the popularity through the eyes of your teen? How are these views similar or different?
- What are your rules and boundaries for social media? Screen time?
- What is your philosophy on privacy as it relates to your teen's phone?
- Have you used applications that limit phone usage or block certain sites? What has been successful and unsuccessful?
- When it comes to experimenting with drugs and alcohol, what are you expecting from your teen?
- When it comes to drugs and alcohol, what are your rules and boundaries? How do you communicate those boundaries to your teen?
- What do you think of peer pressure? How do you think peer pressure plays a role in your teen's life?
- Share a positive conversation you had with your teen about drugs, alcohol, and/or sex and dating. What made the conversation go well?

ACADEMIC WORLD

- When it comes to academics, what is your biggest challenge with your teen?
- What is your teen's greatest academic challenge?
- What is your view of academic pressure? Where is it helpful? Where is it harmful? How do you balance encouragement and pushing? How do you balance helping your teen with encouraging independent thinking/problem-solving?
- How have/do you help your teen overcome procrastination?
- Describe your teen's academic support system.
- When it comes to academic support, what role do you think parents should play in middle school? In high school?
- What are your academic expectations for your teen? What are your teen's academic expectations? Are they aligned? If not, how can you make them more aligned?

PERSONAL GROWTH

- Talk about perfectionism. What role does it play in your life? In the lives of your adult friends? What role does it play in your teen's life? In her friends' lives?
- Who are your teen's positive role models? What qualities do these people model? How?
- What are the top five qualities you respect and admire in your teen? How do you show her you respect those qualities?
- Talk about when and how you discovered your passion. How can this experience help you coach your teen toward uncovering her passion?
- What has been the most challenging change? How have you guided your teen through that change? What was successful? What was unsuccessful? Since that experience, what do you now know about supporting your teen through change?
- Are leadership skills important? Why or why not?
- In what ways do you see teens taking on leadership roles?

-133-

TOOLS FOR LIFE

- What does responsibility mean to you? What do you think it means to your teen?
- How have you been successful in instilling a sense of responsibility in your teen? What were the keys to your success?
- What are typical rules and consequences in your household? Which of those have you found successful and which unsuccessful?
- How do you see the differences between grit and resilience?
- Do you feel you have a resilient teen?
- How have you intentionally cultivated resilience in your teen?
- Where is it easy for you to let go? Where is it harder? Can you identify places where you can let go, but haven't yet?
- What role does compassion and gratitude play in your family?
- How do you promote self-compassion for yourself? For your teen?

References and Resources:

Self-Awareness:

- About Enneagram
  https://www.enneagraminstitute.com/how-the-enneagram-system-works/
- Enneagram quiz
  https://enneagramtest.net/
- VIA Character Strengths test
  https://www.viacharacter.org/survey/account/register
- Spark is a term coined by Dr. Peter Benson, founder of the Search Institute and a leading expert on adolescence. To read more about Sparks, visit:
  https://www.search-institute.org/our-research/youth-development-research/sparks-and-thriving/

Drugs and Alcohol:

- Web MD
  https://www.webmd.com/parenting/features/teen-drug-slang-dictionary-for-parents#1
- National Institute on Drug Abuse
  https://teens.drugabuse.gov/blog/post/molly-spice-and-orange-crush-slang-dangerous-drugs

Time Management:

- https://www.commonsensemedia.org/blog/7-apps-to-help-your-kid-be-more-responsible
- http://www.huffingtonpost.com/brad-spirrison/the-best-apps-for-student_b_3931753.html

Technology:

- Common Sense Media
  https://www.commonsensemedia.org/blog/16-apps-and-websites-kids-are-heading-to-after-facebook#Instagram

References for Adults:

- Bradley, Michael J. *Yes, Your Teen is Crazy! Loving Your Teen Without Losing Your Mind.* Washington: Harbor Press, Inc., 2002.
- Coloroso, Barbara. *The Bully, the Bullied and the Bystander: From Pre-School to High School – How Parents and Teachers Can Help Break the Cycle of Violence.* New York: Harper Collins, 2003.
- Dellasega, Cheryl and Charisse Nixon, Ph.D. *Girl Wars-12 Strategies that Will End Female Bullying.* New York: Simon and Schuster, 2003.
- Damour, Lisa. *Untangled: Guiding Teenage Girls Through the Seven Transitions into Adulthood.* New York: Ballantine Books, 2017.
- Damour, Lisa, Ph.D. *Under Pressure: Confronting the Epidemic of Stress and Anxiety in Girls.* New York: Ballantine Books, 2020.
- Farber, Adele and Elaine Mazlish. *How to Talk So Teens Will Listen & Listen So Teens Will Talk.* New York: Harper Collins, 1980.
- Jensen, Frances E. *The Teenage Brain: A Neuroscientist's Survival Guide to Raising Adolescents and Young Adults.* New York: Harper, 2015.
- Lythcott-Haims, Julie. *How to Raise an Adult: Break Free of the Overparenting Trap and Prepare Your Kid for Success.* New York: Henry Holt and Co., 2015.
- Kilpatrick, Haley. *The Drama Years: Real Girls Talk About Surviving Middle School--Bullies, Brands, Body Image, and More.* New York: Free Press, 2012.
- Siegal, Daniel. *Brainstorm: The Power and Purpose of the Teenage Brain.* New York: TarcherPerigee, 2014.
- Simmons, Rachel. *Odd Girl Out: The Hidden Culture of Aggression in Girls.* New York: Harcourt, Inc., 2002.
- Townsend, John. *Boundaries With Teens: When to say Yes, How to Say No.* Michigan: Zondervan, 2006.
- Wiseman, Rosalind. *Queen Bees & Wannabes: Helping Your Daughter Survive Cliques, Gossip, Boyfriends, and the New Realities of Girl World.* California: Three Rivers Press, 2009.

In-depth 4114U Concepts:

Section 1: Staying Connected

Page 11: Understanding
Page 13: Accountability
Page 13: Boundaries and Expectations
Page 13: Open-Ended Questions
Page 14: Respect
Page 15: Listening

Section 2: Social World

Page 21: Covert Aggression and "Girl Drama"
Page 21: Friendships
Page 22: Conflict Resolution
Page 23: Social Resilience
Page 24: Bullying and Cyberbullying
Page 24: Exclusion
Page 24: Gossip
Page 25: Individuality
Page 25: Social Media
Page 25: Self-Esteem
Page 26: Competence
Page 26: Confidence
Page 27: Empathy
Page 27: Self-Advocacy
Page 28: Popularity
Page 29: Strength and Values
Page 32: Screen Time
Page 35: Reacting versus Responding
Page 38: Alcohol, Tobacco, and Drugs
Page 38: Peer Pressure
Page 39: Decision-Making Skills
Page 41: Inner Strength

Section 3: Academic World

Page 47: Procrastination
Page 47: Motivation
Page 47: Failure
Page 48: Study Skills
Page 48: Time Management
Page 49: Mindset
Page 50: Feeling Stuck
Page 50: Scaffolding for Success
Page 51: Create Support Team
Page 53: Anxiety and Stress
Page 58: Reframe Failure

Section 4: Personal Growth

Page 63: Self-Esteem
Page 63: Perfectionism
Page 63: Comparison
Page 64: Self-Doubt and Self-Criticism
Page 67: Authenticity
Page 71: Passion and Spark
Page 75: Change
Page 78: Leadership
Page 80: Paradigms and Perceptions
Page 80: Habits
Page 85: Responsibility
Page 88: Grit and Resilience
Page 88: Self-Talk
Page 91: Compassion
Page 93: Gratitude

Chapter Books by Reflections Publishing:

BEEP!: Navigating Through ADHD
P: ISBN: 978-1-61660-013-6
Written & Illustrated by: Garrett Ritchie
4114U Illustrations: Julia Paul-Fisher

Crash: Overcoming Fear and Trauma
P: ISBN: 978-1-61660-006-8
Written by: Max Greenhalgh
Illustrated by: Jessa Weiner

Face 2 Face: Navigating Through Cyberbullying, Peer Abuse, & Bullying
P: ISBN: 978-1-61660-002-0
Written by: Caroline Ster
Illustrated by: Emily Jones

Falling to Pieces: Navigating The Transition to Middle School and Merging Friends
P: ISBN: 978-1-61660-007-5
Written by: Sarina Rogers
Illustrated by: Mia Rogers

The Real Beauty: Navigating Through Divorce and Moving
P: ISBN: 978-1-61660-000-6
Written by: Kathryn Mohr
Illustrated by: Kiana Aryan

Scars: Navigating Through Peer Pressure & Consequences of Actions
P: ISBN: 978-1-61660-003-7
By Parent/Child Team: Dave, Julian, and Noelle Franco

Shining Through a Social Storm: Navigating Through Relational Aggression, Bullying, and Popularity
P: ISBN: 978-1-61660-004-4
Written by: Skylar Sorkin
Illustrated by: Sydney Green

Graphic Novel by Reflections Publishing:

Jasper and the Spirit Skies: Volume 1
P: ISBN 978-1-61660-015-0
Written and Illustrated by:
Canyon Crest Academy's Envision Conservatory for the Humanities and Envision Visual Arts Conservatory

Picture Books by Reflections Publishing:

Remind Me Again: Navigating Through the Loss of a Loved One
HC: ISBN: 978-1-61660-001-3
P: ISBN: 978-1-61660-010-5
Written by: The Ster Family
Illustrated by: Colleen C. Ster

A Mother's Love: Overcoming a Disability and Believing in Yourself
HC: ISBN: 978-1-61660-011-2
P: ISBN: 978-1-61660-008-2
Written by: Anthony Mazza
and Emmanuel Ofosu Yeboah

Remember Me When: Navigating Through Alzheimer's Disease
HC: ISBN: 978-1-61660-0012-9
P: ISBN: 978-1-61660-009-9
Written by: Isabelle Ster
Illustrated by: Emily Morgan

**Books Available through:
ReflectionsPublishing.com, Amazon.com,
Follett Library Resources, Barnes and Noble,
Baker and Taylor, and Ingram.**

www.ingramcontent.com/pod-product-compliance
Lightning Source LLC
Chambersburg PA
CBHW070812100426
42742CB00012B/2339